SUPER DUPER SUPERMEN!

COMIC BOOK HEROES FROM THE FORTIES AND FIFTIES!

A DENIS GIFFORD COLLECTION

GREENWOOD

A GREEN WOOD BOOK
COPYRIGHT © 1991 THE GREEN WOOD PUBLISHING COMPANY LTD

COPYRIGHT © 1992 TEXT AND COMPILATION DENIS GIFFORD

COPYRIGHT © COMICS: VARIOUS PUBLISHING COMPANIES AS LISTED.

ALL RIGHTS RESERVED. NO PART OF THIS PUBLICATION MAY BE REPRODUCED, STORED IN A RETRIEVAL SYSTEM OR TRANSMITTED IN ANY FORM BY ANY MEANS, ELECTRONIC, MECHANICAL, PHOTO-COPYING, RECORDING OR OTHERWISE, WITHOUT THE PERMISSION OF THE COPYRIGHT HOLDER.

ISBN 1 872532 84 5

PHOTOGRAPHY BY DEREK SMITH AND JAY TAUBEN

DESIGN BY TITAN STUDIO

TYPESET IN GREAT BRITAIN BY TITAN STUDIO

PRINTED AND BOUND IN HONG KONG

THE GREEN WOOD PUBLISHING COMPANY LTD
6/7 WARREN MEWS
LONDON W1P 5DJ

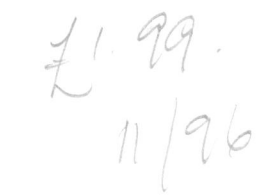

CONTENTS

Introduction:
Those Super Duper Sixpennies!

Robert Lovett: Back from the Dead

Krakos: The Egyptian

Halcon: Lord of the Crater-Land

Powerman

Crash Britanus: World Crime Buster

Streamline:
The Fastest Fighter in the World

Tola the Strong

Speed Gale and Garry: Super 'Tecs

Electro-Girl

Superboyo

Ju-Jitsu Jimmy

Maxwell the Mighty:
The 1000 HP Human

Marsman

Zom of the Zodiac

Litening: The Son of the Gods

Quicksilver:
The Wonderman of the West

Ace Hart: The Atom Man

Super Thriller Annual

Maskman

Captain Crash: Dynamic Wonder

Wonderman: The Atomic Marvel

The Tornado

Atom: The Mighty Boy

Ray Spede: The Rocket Man

Gail Garrity: Girl Wonder

Captain Might: The Nemesis of Crime

Captain Magnet

Captain Zenith

Electroman

Mr Apollo

Masterman

Captain Vigour: Strongman of Sport

Steve Samson:
Strong Man of the Circus

Superstooge

Captain Universe: The Super Marvel

Marvelman:
The Mightiest Man in the Universe

Marvelman at War

Marvelman Annual

Young Marvelman:
The Mightiest Boy in the Universe

Young Marvelman Annual

Marvelman Family:
The Mightiest Family in the Universe

Marvelman Family Annual

Captain Miracle

The Purple Hood:
Crime Fighter International

Mark Tyme:
The Fantastic Time Traveller

THOSE SUPER-DUPER SIXPENNIES!

One silver sixpence, that was the admission charge for a handful of thrills so super, in fact so super-duper, back in those fabulous Fifties. It was an era of entertainment for youngsters that has seldom been bettered as far as unfettered fun and adventure goes. A comic-book era when, as one company claimed, 'Sports Cartoons Comics are written by British authors, illustrated by British artists, designed for British readers!' It was also an era when another comic-book company, equally lively and exciting in its product, could try to pass off their wares as genoowine Yankee, right down to the fake price of Ten Cents on their covers!

British comic-books began early in 1940 about a month after the last distribution of American comic-books to the nation's newsagents and market stalls. These had been readily available here since *Famous Funnies* first appeared back in 1933, and yours truly, the tyro comic artist, had been spending his every spare threepence on them right through the Thirties. Suddenly we were at war, and there were more important things to ship to Britain than remaindered comic-books from the USA.

One man saved the youth of these islands from withdrawal symptoms. Gerald G. Swan, market stall-owner, wholesaler of American comics and magazines, and a man of foresight, acumen and inspiration. Realising he would no longer have Yankee comic-books to distribute to his comic-hungry readers, Gerald G. Swan recognised the hole in the market and promptly filled it. He became a comic-book editor and publisher. He it was who invented the first ever British comic-book, and called it *New Funnies*. Modelled closely on its transatlantic forbears, *New Funnies* No. 1, dated February 1940, had sixty-four pages of pictures stapled into a full colour cover, all for sixpence. The interior had to be black-and-white; full colour would have been too much to ask for in blitzed Britain. And it had to cost sixpence, rather a lot to ask in a day when the regular British comics cost but a penny or twopence. But to comic-book starved kids, it was a wonder: the biggest comic ever published in the UK.

New Funnies was soon followed by more titles, a new one every month, – *Topical Funnies, War Comics, Thrill Comics, Slick Fun, Fresh Fun, Extra Fun* – until the new paper controls and rationing put a stop to the landslide. As it happened, Swan had been just in time. His avalanche of comic-books each acquired a paper quota and was able to sustain publication right through the war. Well, all except *Extra Fun*, but even that tail-end Charlie was able to stage a comeback in later years.

The style and content of Swan's comic-books was curious, a slightly uneasy blend of American and traditional English, due perhaps to its being drawn by mostly veteran cartoonists unable to sustain regular work for the mainline publishers. This gave rise to the unique aura Swan comics have for those brought up on them, a special nostalgia still felt by the evacuated generation of the Second

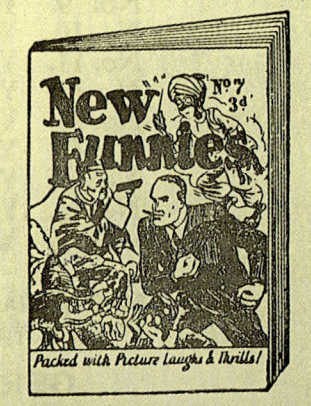

World War. Swan used all manner of strips, from slapstick to supernatural, and one or two of his weirdest find a place in this review of super-heroes. 'Back from the Dead', the ongoing tale of Robert Lovett, animated corpse dead lo these hundred or more years, and revived by a grave-robber with amazing powers. 'Krakos the Egyptian', an age-old near-mummy who rejuvenates to fly to London – without an aeroplane! – and set Nazis afire en route. These are two who paved the way for more traditional American-style super-heroes.

Swan brought his comic-books down in size and price: threepence for twenty pages or so. A. Soloway, however, preferred a classier comic-book closer perhaps to the traditional. His books cost fourpence for sixteen pages, and they were all two-coloured throughout. Nat Brand, one of our 'lost' artists, drew much for Soloway, from 'Halcon, Lord of the Crater-land', a Tarzan type, to 'Crash Carew, Daredevil of the Stratosphere' (who may be found in our companion volume, *Space Aces!*). Brand drew close to the Alex Raymond-Flash Gordon archetype, but with enough nib-dash of his own to make one want to know more about him.

Cartoon Art Productions were the odd Glaswegian outfit who priced all their comics in cents. Dennis M. Reader and Crewe Davies were their great discoveries, both drawing their utmost in the approved Yankee style. Later came Paget Publications (a Mr Usher of Netheravon Road), and the science-fiction paperback publishers, Scion Ltd, of Kensington. The former introduced Mick Anglo art to the world, the latter the brilliant brush technique of Ron Turner. In fact, many were the young chaps of the post-war breed of penmen that made their debuts in these threepenny and sixpenny comic-books: Don Lawrence on Marvelman, Ron Embleton on Litening, Bob Monkhouse on Tornado, (yes, *that* Bob Monkhouse!). Even I started on super-heroes, way back at the age of seventeen, producing *Dynamic Comics*, a tuppeny eight-pager starring 'Mr Muscle – Britain's Superman!' Terrible stuff, but training, I suppose, for my later work on the Marvelman team.

The sixpenny comic-book had its heyday during the period when a well meaning government banned the importation of American comic-books into the UK. Reprint editions of American comics flourished, backed by those British comics, by British artists, for British readers, of whom we spoke earlier. But once full-colour American comic-books returned, our native stuff had very little chance of survival. The publishers disappeared, the artists moved on to better things, and it was, as they say, the End of an Era.

ROBERT LOVETT: BACK FROM THE DEAD

by William McCail
War Comics (1940) *Topical Funnies* (1941) *Picture Epics* (1952)
Gerald G. Swan Ltd (London)

'As the grave robber filed at the rings on Robert Lovett's fingers, the dead man's hand slowly started to grip him. With a horrible scream the burglar sank to the floor of the vault. Robert Lovett had awakened!' The strangest super-hero of them all – a corpse revived after 113 years in the family vault – in the strangest costume of all – a flat cap and an upturned raincoat! Such was Robert Lovett, entombed on November the first 1827, revived November 1940 in No. 5 of *War Comics*. Soon the walking corpse discovers he has the power to see through walls. He follows a fanatical-looking neighbour to the City Water Supply, overhearing his cry of 'We shall be revenged! This tube will carry millions of germs into London's water supply and cause disease to our enemies! Gott strafe England!' Not knowing England is at war with Germany, Lovett cries, 'Oh, I wish I could kill that madman!' Instantly there is a terrific flash of lightning, and the Nazi spy pitches forward with a dreadful cry, and lies still. 'I possess the power to kill at wish and see through solids!' muses the man from the dead, stroking his hollow cheeks thoughtfully. 'I can be all powerful!' And in succeeding episodes, with the steel-like grip of his claw-like hands, and lightning flashing from his fiery eyes, he embarks on 'a ruthless war against the foulest type of criminal'.

The macabre series, laced with levity, was a popular thriller in blitzed Britain. A decade after it concluded, Bill McCail's talented artist brother, John, compiled it into a fifty-two-page comic-book, *Picture Epics No. 1*, and drew the striking coloured cover.

THE SPINE-CHILLING SAGA OF A MAN WHO CAME—
BACK FROM THE DEAD
1/-
ROBERT LOVETT
DIED 1827
CAME BACK 1949
PICTURE EPICS
No. 1

KRAKOS: THE EGYPTIAN
by William Ward
New Funnies (1941) *Thrill Comics* (1942)
Gerald G. Swan Ltd (London)

'O Tanis!' muttered the doddering old man as he entered the Great Pyramid, 'give me strength to reach your secret tomb and burn the sacred herbs! My palsied hands can scarcely strike the fatal match!' But they did, and from the blaze arose a clean-limbed young Egyptian crying 'It is accomplished, O Tanis! Thine ancient lore is realised!' Changing his traditional native costume for a snap-brimmed fedora, double-breasted mac and a cigarette in a long holder, he says 'I can arrive at London now without attracting too much attention!' – and immediately flies through the skies without an aeroplane! En route he explodes the rifles of a Nazi firing squad. 'Who are you?' asks the astounded officer. 'Nemesis to you, worshipper of stone gods!' says Krakos the Egyptian, setting the officer on fire with a touch. 'The angel of the burning death walks among you!' And it is off to London where his servant, Yusef, and a great house awaits him, along with many a murky crime around the fogbound waterfront.

William Ward, once an animator on the popular *Bonzo* cartoon films, found a new career in the comic-books published by Gerald G. Swan during World War Two. His animation techniques often showed through the fog and fantasy of the six-page picture stories he favoured, adding an odd touch of comedy to his gothic horrors.

SPECIAL SPRING NUMBER
THRILL
6D
COMICS
THRILLS, FUN & LAUGHTER

HALCON: LORD OF THE CRATER-LAND
by Nat Brand
Comic Capers (1942) *Halcon Comics* (1948) *Splendid Book for Boys* (c.1955)
A. Soloway Ltd (London) Collins (Glasgow)

Halcon, whose name rhymes with 'falcon', was a blond Tarzan type who roamed the deserts and jungles of the untamed Crater-Land with little more than a loincloth and red waistcoat to protect him against sandstorms, wildlife, Nazi paratroopers and Arab slave-traders. With dialogue seldom exceeding the occasional expletive 'Bwantu!', the accent was on excellently drawn action with the occasional touch of sex, all a growing boy could ask for in those dark days of World War Two. In a sequence of episodes unusual in British comics, Halcon saved a lovely white women, Karen, from a tribe of nomadic slavers just as they were about to sacrifice her to a man-eating plant. He carried her by camel to his jungle abode, the 'shelter-tree', where they snuggled beneath the leaves until the next issue of *Comic Capers*.

Nat Brand is one of the great lost artists of British adventure strips. His creations included Crash Carew, Daredevil of the Stratosphere; Bentley Price, Private Detective; and Dandy McQueen of the Royal Mounted. All efforts to locate him have failed, and it may be that his name was a pseudonym. His work was mainly for the Soloway group of comics, which also included *Comic Adventures, All Star* and *All Fun*.

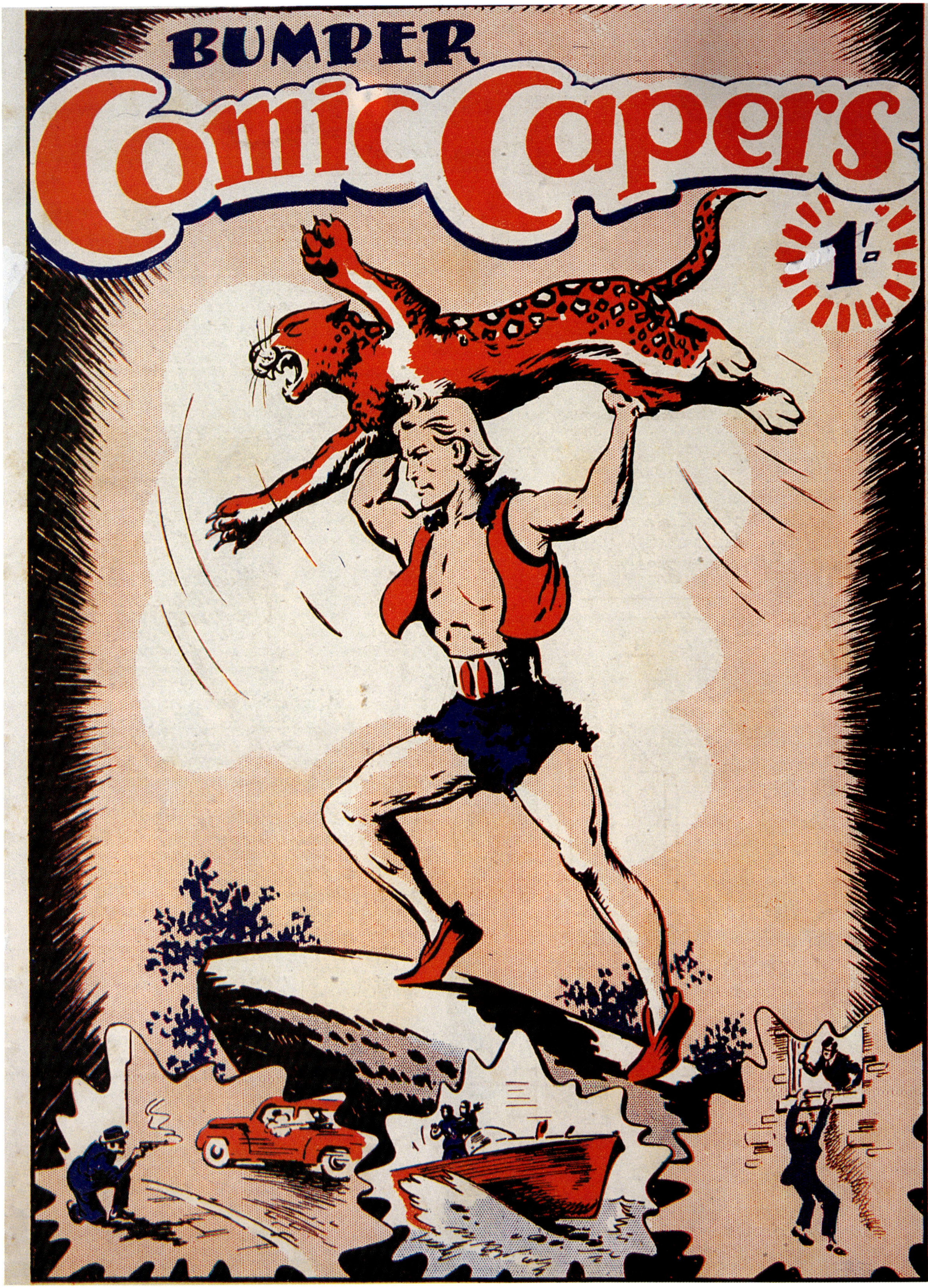
BUMPER
Comic Capers
1/-

POWERMAN
by Dennis M. Reader
Super Duper Comics **(1946)**
Cartoon Art Productions (Glasgow)

Powerman made his dynamic debut on the front page of *Super Duper Double Decker Adventure and Funster Comic* No. 3. Or did he? On other copies of the same comic, Johnny Service, better known as Crime Busting Incognito, was the front page star! This unique mystery in the history of British comics has never been solved, but of the two heroes, Powerman survived the longer run of super-adventures. 'Our story opens on Christmas Eve in a city in Illinois, the apartment of Kerry Lattimer, Britisher and Crime Reporter.' Enter an aged gent whose tall topper shadows his face. He gives Kerry a 'seasonal present from the mists of time', a copy of Dickens's *Christmas Carol*! Opening the book, Kerry hears a *Bam!* and out pops a shrouded figure. 'I am the ghost of Christmas yet to come! I bear a message. On the dawn of Christmas Day you will become a crime fighting force endowed with super-human gifts! Be prepared! Use this strength and wisdom to bring about good in this upset world! Farewell!' And as Christmas Day dawned, so dawned a new Kerry – Powerman! Complete with cloak, mask and a big 'P' for his chest. His beat ranged from Ohio to Harlem, and his opponents included the wicked Vampire Lady, assisted by sundry robots and zombies.

Dennis M. Reader ('I added the "M" because it sounded more American!') was a left-handed teenager in love with American comic-books. His many characters for Cartoon Art comics included Burt Steele and Satin Astro, Wonder Boy, Electro-Girl, and the cowboy Dusty Trale.

SUPER-DUPER
No.
CAP-TOON
10¢
FEATURE
Cartoon Art
6D
Productions
NEW ADVENTURE and
FUNSTER COMIC
THRILLS
SUSPENS
ACTION
STARRING
POWER-MAN !
and
JOHNNY SERVICE
SHYBOLD KID
and
FUNNIES
Features
DENNIS M. READER

CRASH BRITANUS: WORLD CRIME BUSTER

by Crewe Davies
Crasho Comic No. 1 (1947)
W. Daly (Manchester)

'Many thousands of years ago, before the Earth was inhabited, this world of ours was in the direct path of a meteorite bearing strange forms of living matter. It landed at a point now known as Central Africa, and so started a small group of humans on this planet.' In 1920 an English missionary found a small child wandering in the jungle. Not knowing he was a descendant through a line of Chieftains to the first man on Earth, he took the infant home where, through his prowess at sport, he was nicknamed 'Crash'. In 1940 Crash joined the Intelligence and was in the centre of Hiroshima when the Atom Bomb dropped. 'Nuclear fusion gave us the World Crime Buster!' complete with mask, uniform and the emblem 'B'! Crash promptly celebrated by looping the loop around the plane that dropped the bomb! Demobbed in 1946, Crash tunes his ears into a telephone conversation and hears that Val, a scientist's assistant, has been kidnapped from her bedroom for the secret of a fuel 100 times more powerful than petrol. Evil Dr Ching takes her by rocket to his City in the Clouds, staffed by robots with human brains. But Crash flies to the rescue (he needs no plane) and destroys the City by cutting off its support – anti-gravity rays. As a bonus, 'the local farmers will have all the electricity they want!'

Crewe Davies, one of the first comic artists to specialise in sci-fi and super-heroes, had a lively style but suffered from some sort of bad spell. His hero was called Brittanus on the cover, Britanus in the title, and Britunus in the strip!

CRASHO Comic

9ᴰ

Contents:—
"CRASH" BRITTANUS
Curley and his magic slate
Fantastic Facts
Features

STREAMLINE: THE FASTEST FIGHTER IN THE WORLD

by Denis Gifford
Streamline Comics No. 1 (1947)
Cardal Publishing Co (Manchester)

'The Adventure of the Flaming Fiends' opens with a fiery inferno: the 21st National Bank is burning down. Scientist Keenan King is on the spot and suspicious. Back in his laboratory King pulls off his shirt and jabs his arm with a dose of – 'Ouch!' – Elixir X! 'Keenan King has spent eighteen months perfecting this new drug. We cannot give a detailed and scientific explanation here, but if it works – and it does work! – suffice to say Keenan is now the Fastest Man Alive!' Evidently King has studied super-hero form, to judge by his next speech balloon: 'The first thing to do is to get a skin-tight uniform. Everyday clothes are too cumbersome. And I must think up a title for myself!' And thus is born Streamline, Speediest Crimefighter in the World! King is as fast in his lab as he is on his feet, for quickly whipping up a liquid that dissolves asbestos, he deprives the bank-busters of their protective suits and splats them through the flames to safe custody. As one conked crook remarks, 'Groan! I don't believe it even now!'

    A complete comic-book drawn over a weekend as Duty Clerk by Denis Gifford, AC1 Clerk/Pay Accounts. Other characters included a serial, 'The Search for the Secret City', 'Bully Beef' and a burlesque on the super-hero genre, 'Super Worm'. *Streamline Comics* ran for four monthly issues, the final adventure of Keenan King being drawn by Bryan Berry, who was later to become a much admired science-fiction novelist.

STARRING STREAMLINE!!
STREAMLINE
Comics
No. 1.
SPLAT
6d.
DENIS GIFFORD 47
ACTION AND THRILLS BURSTING from EVERY PICTURE!

TOLA THE STRONG
by W. Forshaw
Ensign Comic No. 1 (1947)
Ensign Publishing Co (Liverpool)

'This is a story of ancient Turkey and a mighty warrior who rides a winged horse, Tola the Strong, an enemy feared by all who live in defiance of law and order.' Chief Kemil climbs up to Tola's mountain cave with a tale of how Hamed the Sultan has carried off Karma, his daughter, intending to wed her. Tola mounts his noble steed, Red Cloud, and literally flies to her rescue – Red Cloud is a winged horse! Carving a bloody way through the castle guards, thanks to his mighty sword and a red/green printing process, Tola finds himself trapped in a Torture Hall with a superbly drawn tiger. After an unusually long and visual battle (no fewer than nine panels), Tola wins out and thwarts the evil Sultan, thanks to the lovely Karma and her unexpected muscles.

W. Forshaw was artist, editor and publisher of several short-lived comics issued from his home at Barry Street, Liverpool. Printer of this curiously coloured comic was Eric Bemrose, not yet the full colour photogravure fashioner of the famous *Eagle*. *Ensign* ran for four issues, each starring a variety of comic characters.

THE COMIC YOU HAVE BEEN WAITING FOR!

ENSIGN COMIC 3D

TOLA THE STRONG

THIS IS A STORY OF ANCIENT TURKEY AND OF A MIGHTY WARRIOR WHO RIDES A WINGED HORSE, TOLA THE STRONG, AN ENEMY FEARED BY ALL WHO LIVE IN DEFIANCE OF LAW AND ORDER.

THREE MEN WEARILY CLIMB A MOUNTAIN TOWARDS A CAVE.

"I SAVED YOUR LIFE MANY MOONS AGO AND YOU PROMISED YOUR AID IF EVER I WAS IN NEED OF IT!"

"I REMEMBER, O CHIEF KEMIL!"

"HAMED THE SULTAN HAS CARRIED AWAY KARMA MY DAUGHTER! I AM A POOR CHIEFTAIN. HOW CAN I FIGHT AGAINST HIM?"

"TOO LONG HAS HAMED HELD SWAY. GO BACK TO YOUR PEOPLE! LEAVE THIS MATTER WITH ME!"

"COME, RED CLOUD, WE HAVE WORK TO DO!"

SPEED GALE AND GARRY : SUPER 'TECS

Super Duper Comics (1947) *Speed Gale Comics* (1947)
Cartoon Art Productions (Glasgow)

Speed Gale sits in his laboratory night after night, waiting for a call on his Super-Selective Radio Transmitter. At last it comes : the Atomic Gang is breaking into the National Bank! Garry, Gale's young assistant, makes a well-timed dash through the door and soon the pair are donning skin-tight suits and quaffing 'from flasks which contain a liquid elixir that is Speed Gale's own discovery – it gives them mastery over the air and super-human strength!' The pair take off from the flat-topped roof of their quarters, England's perfect answer to Batman and Robin! They descend onto the roof of the stricken bank building and Speed drops through the skylight into the automatically wrecked strongroom. Pulling out 'his cunningly concealed patent gun', he cries, 'Put 'em up, boys!' But one of the boys has a mystery weapon of his own. 'Speed is conscious of a shock and a paralysing numbness … a blackout passes over his brain!' Speed is kidnapped in a flying car, but luckily sidekick Garry takes to the air, too, and gives chase. In an underground palace Speed comes face to face with the fanatical Magram, who has the hero tortured to obtain the secret of flight. The electrical current restores Speed's superhuman strength, and the atomic fanatic is swiftly done for. 'That concludes another case successfully, boss!' laughs Garry, as he arrives with the Flying Squad.

Speed Gale was drawn by an anonymous local cartoonist who provided most of this Scottish publisher's early comics. He could turn his pen to many types of adventure, including Daredevil Denver, who roamed the old west on Fireball, his wonder horse.

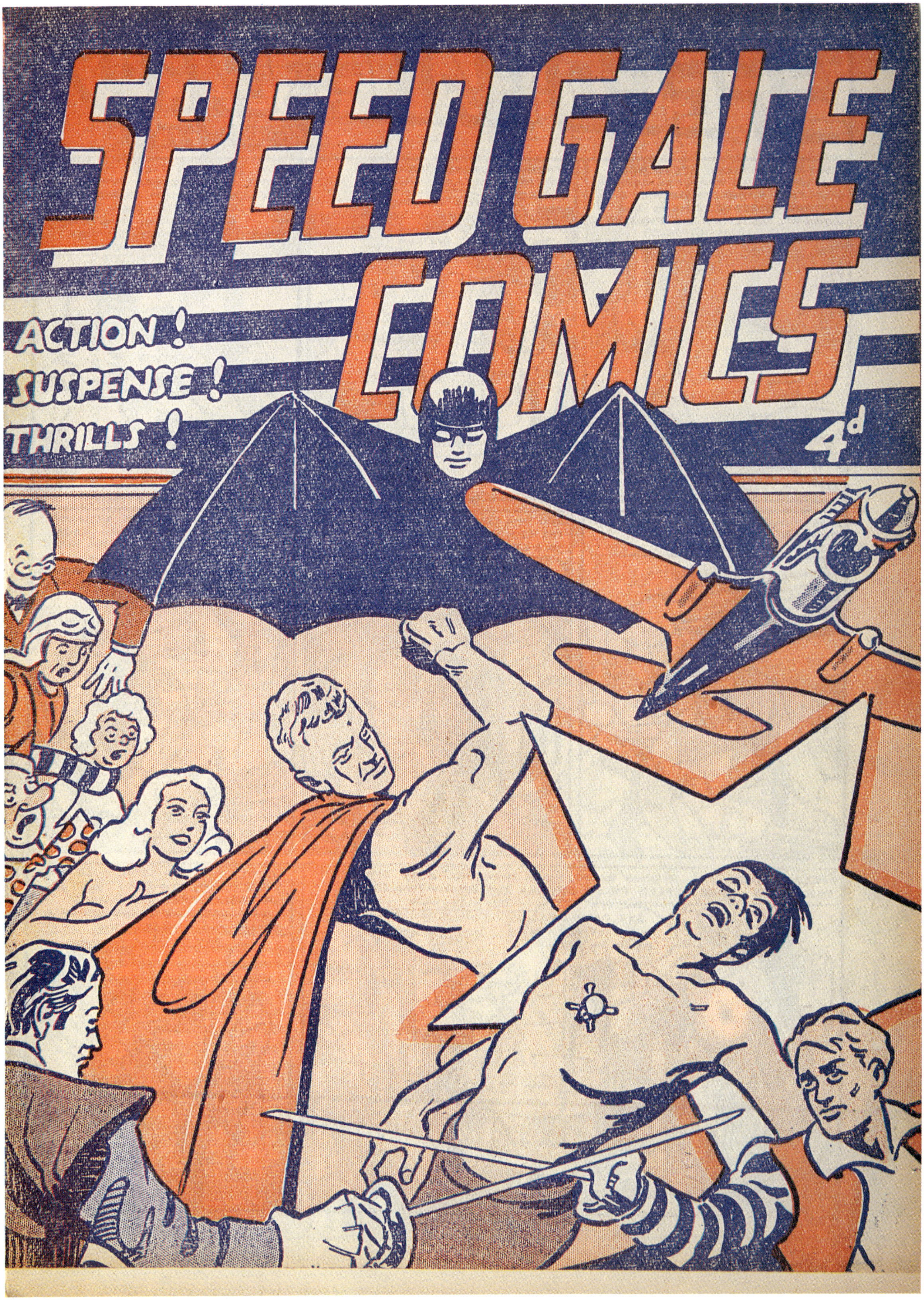
SPEED GALE COMICS
ACTION!
SUSPENSE!
THRILLS!
4d

ELECTRO-GIRL
by Dennis M. Reader
Whizzer Comics **(1947)** *Super Duper Comics* **(1947)**
Cartoon Art Productions (Glasgow)

'Hello, boys and gals!' she said, opening her first chapter, 'The Slap-Happy Safe Crackers', 'Here's where I smash into my first adventure!' This was Electro-Girl, cloaked alter-ego of Carol Flane, daughter of the eminent electro-biologist. 'Here is the story of the creation and outcome of a crime-fighting force, a gal who strikes terror into the hearts of the minions of evil!' Entering her dead dad's lab, Carol fingers the dials of his last experiment. 'Abruptly there is a terrific bolt of electricity and Carol is thrown high into the charged air!' An hour later she revives, strokes Buster the kitten, and kills it stone dead! 'I'm radiating a powerful electric force!' cries Carol amid several *'Zaps'*. Three weeks later a trio of plug-uglies meet in a cellar to read the local paper. In it is an ad : 'To whom it may concern! I, Electro-Girl, will give no peace to law-breakers. Take heed, all wrong-doers.' This leads to much laughter. 'Haw-haw! A dame scares us!' cackle the crooks, but no sooner are they robbing the Realm Bank than Electro-Girl, on a nocturnal prowl, shoots them down with lightning bolts radiating from her fingers. 'Awk!' cries the gang boss, 'The dame's a walkin' generator!'

Electro-Girl, or Gal as creator Dennis M. Reader might well have called her, was one of several super-women the Yank-struck cartoonist devised. There was Cat-Girl in Swan's *Thrill Comics* (1946), and Acromaid for Cartoon Art Productions, plus several lady side-kicks to his

No. 5
SUPER-DUPER
GREAT BRITAIN
NEW ADVENTURE and
FUNSTER
COMIC
CARTOON FEATURE
10¢
introducing
ELECTRO GIRL
POWERMAN!
in
THE Adventure
of the
"KRAZY KRIME"
SKYBOLT KID &
HIS JET-PLANE
DENNIS M. READER

SUPERBOYO
by Rex Hart
The Three-Star Adventures (1947) *The Atom* (1947)
R. Turvey (London)

This strange tale begins with young Alan Brent being taken on a mysterious quest by his guardian, scientist Sir Hugo Dunn. Taken by plane to Kairuan, the pair entrain for the Unknown Land of White Crags, a journey that includes several weeks drive by safari car, followed by a ride in a camel caravan, by canoe through the jungle belt, carriage by native boys, and finally by foot up the snowbound mountains. Sir Hugo grows weaker and tells Alan to cross Table Mountain to a magic pool where a short swim will turn him into a superman! Suddenly a Flying Wing swoops low, and a burst of machine-gun fire kills the old gentleman. Alan makes a tomb of rocks for him, vowing to avenge him one day. Then the tropic moon rises and the flying wing returns. Bullets fly, and Alan dives to escape them. Then, 'in the pool Superboyo feels himself the centre of powerful radiations. 'Great Heavens!' he cries, 'What's happening? An earthquake? Or Magic? shall I ever escape? Wish I could fly out like a plane!' And he promptly does! Alan flies off after the Wing and learns that it is controlled by a dark-skinned man. Alan calls him 'Inkyface', but he is the would-be dictator of the world, the only man with the secret of the Supratomic Bomb!

Superboyo has two major claims to fame : he is the only super-hero to fly without a super-costume – shirt and long trousers are good enough for him – and he suffers with the silliest name ever coined. His comic, a three-colour job printed by Foldes Press of Edinburgh, was distributed by David Overend of Glasgow. The costume was put right in his second adventure, which appears in a comic called *The Atom*. He was given a flowing red cloak with jacket and tights to match.

THE 3-STAR ADVENTURES
4d
SLEUTH JONES, REPORTER.
RANCHO ALERT.
SUPER-BOYO.
ALAN BRENT IS BEING TAKEN ON A MYSTERIOUS QUEST BY HIS GUARDIAN, SIR HUGO DUNN, THE SCIENTIST---
IN THEIR PRIVATE PLANE A DANGEROUS STOWAWAY SUDDENLY SHOWS HIMSELF--
THIS IS YOUR EXIT, GENTS! TOO BAD YOU AIN'T GOT NO 'CHUTES! -JUST THE SAME BALE OUT!
OUT YOURSELF!

JU-JITSU JIMMY

By Rex Hart
The Atom **(1947)**
Buchanan Books (London)

Jimmy looked not unlike the sort of chap into whose face a a bully might kick sand! Especially as he stood about a beach in black-and-red striped swimming trunks. However, 'that little squirt won't be no trouble,' muttered a couple of crooks whose eyes were on Rita Gold, heiress, who was taking her diamond necklace for a morning stroll along the sands. But Jimmy had a secret, small as he was. This was the power of Ju-Jitsu, and within two pages packed with swinging action, Ju-Jitsu Jimmy ('Good old JJJ!' as his pals were wont to remark) soon had the crooks crying for the cops, with at least one broken arm apiece.

Rex Hart, who drew this complete twelve-page three-colour comic, seemed to have trouble with the title. Although it is called *The Atom* (the Little Comic with the Big Features), the cover emphasises both Ju-Jitsu and Tarzan as possible titles, too! Rather cunningly, Hart includes a full-page feature entitled 'Holiday with Tarzan'. It begins, 'Tarzan visited London not so long ago, and he gave the Editor an interview especially to introduce this new picture book to all young readers.' There follows a series of exercises young people can do on a seaside beach. Hart seems to have been star-struck : the back page strip includes Claude Dampier, 'Monsewer' Eddie Gray, Bud Flanagan, Sid Field, the Western Brothers and Danny Kaye!

MAKE A TOY BUTTER CHURN AND MAKE REAL CREAM AND BUTTER (SEE INSIDE).
The ATOM
THE LITTLE COMIC WITH THE BIG FEATURES
Starring:-
JU-JITSU
J. J. Jimmy • SUMMER-SLEDGING •
SURF-RIDING • Super Comics •
The MAGIC BOY
Introduced by the real
TARZAN
YOU FLY KITES BUT THIS ONE FLIES YOU - and it's real! see inside.
3d

MAXWELL THE MIGHTY: THE 1000 HP HUMAN
Prang Comic (1948)
Hotspur Publishing Co (Manchester)

Maxwell the Mighty seems to have been the only super-hero in the phonebook. Professor Dent, beset by spies after his secret formula, phones Maxwell just as a bullet lays him low: 'Aagh!' In one minute Maxwell is at the lab, interviewing Mrs Reed, the prof's landlady, and saving his secretary, Miss Dent, from being pitched off a bridge. 'Like a human tornado he catches the girl in mid-air!', landing safely as the night express rushes by. In a split second, super-hero and girl are rushing off to Cheyne House, hideout of the spies. 'We're on our way, my chickadee!' says Maxwell, echoing another sort of super-hero. Maxwell is given to odd exclamations. 'Jemima!' he yells, as he wrestles with a giant python, and 'Cripes!' he cries as he rips up a thousand-volt cable in his bare hands, starting a fire. Bunging a bomb back at a bomb-bunging baddie, Maxwell quickly closes the case: 'Well, that's avenged the professor and burned out a rat's nest!'

Drawn by an anonymous artist who produced the complete eight-page comic, Maxwell the Mighty was backed up by 'The Sky Commando Daredevil Kent Carew', billed as 'Crime-breaker of the Air, Test-pilot and Tec!', plus 'Peter Puck and the Wishing Ring'.

PRANG COMIC 3D
MAXWELL THE MIGHTY
THE 1000 H.P. HUMAN
A LATE NIGHT CALL FROM PROF. DENT SENDS MAXWELL HOT-FOOT TO THE PROF'S LABORATORY
HELLO! MAXWELL HERE!
HELLO!
THIS IS PROF. DENT - SPIES ARE AFTER MY SECRET FORMULA - I AM IN DANGER - AACH!
GOSH! WHAT'S HAPPENED? - SOUNDED LIKE A GUNSHOT!
ONE MINUTE LATER - AT THE LABORATORY MAXWELL SEES MRS. REED, THE PROFESSOR'S LANDLAD
THE SWINE - HE'S KILLED THE PROFESSOR HE WENT THAT WAY - ACROSS THE BRIDGE
TO THE BRIDGE, E FOR PETE'S SAKE THERE'S A SCRAP GOING ON THERE!
THAT'S HIM! AND THERE'S THE PROFESSOR'S SECRETARY, MISS DENT, TRYING TO STOP HIM
HE'S PITCHING HER OVER!
LIKE A HUMAN TORNADO MAXWELL MOVES - HE DIVES OVER THE BRIDGE, AND CATCHES THE GIRL IN MID-AIR

MARSMAN
By Paddy Brennan
Marsman Comics **(1948)**
Cartoon Art Productions (Glasgow)

Star of his own sixpenny comic-book, Marsman flew into Bigburg (USA, of course) near naked but certainly unashamed. Clad only in skullcap, short pants, gloves and boots, he landed atop the Grand Hotel to the amazement of reporters, cops and crooks alike. Marsman's mission: 'I've come to make a report on Earth's social life and civilisation for my planet!' How come he speaks English? 'Simple! We Martians have listened to your radio. I can speak twenty other languages!' Marsman's unexplained lack of transport does not stop a cop charging him with low flying, so the space alien zooms off with a familiar cry of 'Up and away!' His super-heroics are confined to a fairly straightforward capture of Benny the Slug and buddy, involving little more than a game of catch with their lorry-load of loot. Then Marsman is off to the heights of a skyscraper to survey the town he has come to investigate. After thirty-seven superbly drawn pictures, he would be seen no more.

Patrick 'Paddy' Brennan was easily the best of the new post-war breed of comic-book artists, his fine-line work full of both action and humorous humanity. After an apprenticeship in the low-budget comic-books, he went to D.C. Thomson, where he became a top-class staff artist for the rest of his long career.

MARSMAN COMICS

6ᴰ

20 PAGES OF FUN AND ADVENTURE!
IN COLOUR

ZOM OF THE ZODIAC

by S.K. Perkins
Big Win Comic (1948)
Scion Ltd (London)

Zom of the Zodiac is one of the oddest super-heroes to appear in British comics. He arrives on the two-tone scene with remarkably little explanation: 'Zom, the Mystery Man of the Zodiac, has the power to transform human beings into any shape he pleases.' And that's it! Observing a muscle-bound thug clunking a bespectacled wimp and making off with his briefcase, Zom hears the dazed victim mutter, 'I wish I were a big he-man so that I could get back my satchel.' Says Zom, 'If that is what you wish, then so you shall be – arise!' In the next panel the thumped one arises a changed man, even more muscle-bound than the thumper. In next to no time Timkins (later Timpkins!) has bopped the baddie and signed up to star with Rita Hayden in her next movie! Zom grants further strength-enhancing wishes before the strip ends – for ever!

    S.K. Perkins was an old-timer in the comic business, being a contributor to *Comic Life* as far back as 1925 ('Ted of All Tools'). He worked exclusively for the Target Publications comics during the Thirties, where his main claim to fame was the front page picturisations of Harry Hemsley's imaginary radio family, 'Elsie, Winnie and Johnny' for the *Ovaltiney's Own Comic* (1935-8). He did his best to modernise his style in Forties' comic-books, but although always full of movement, his images remained rooted in a traditional past.

BIG WIN COMIC

ZOM OF THE ZODIAC

3D

ZOM, THE MYSTERY MAN OF THE ZODIAC WHO HAS THE POWER TO TRANSFORM HUMAN BEINGS INTO ANY SHAPE HE PLEASES, DECIDES TO HELP TIMPKINS, A MEEK AND UNDERPAID CLERK, TO GET A SQUARE DEAL

"MEET ME AT THE RITZ CINEMA WHERE RITA HAYDEN IS APPEARING AT A PREMIERE — DON'T YOU DARE LOSE THAT SATCHEL!"

"IT'S MINE NOW YOU SKINNY SAP!"

"IF THAT IS WHAT YOU WISH THEN SO YOU SHALL BE — ARISE!"

"I WISH I WERE A BIG HE-MAN SO THAT I COULD GET BACK MY SATCHEL"

"POOR LITTLE FISH"

"WHY, I HAVE CHANGED INTO ONE!"

"I'LL SOON GET MY SATCHEL BACK!"

LITENING: THE SON OF THE GODS
by Ronald Embleton
Big Flame Wonder Comic **(1948)**
Scion Ltd (London)

This 'story of a young man who was favoured by the Gods to combat the forces of Evil' begins with an old man who watches and waits. He observes young David Terry saving a cat from the jaws of a stray dog, and cries, 'You are the man I have been looking for, a man with goodness in his heart, and the courage to pit his strength against the forces of evil! Come!' In a daze, Dave follows the old man 'through clouds of swirling vapour to the home of the Gods, where he is given great powers to aid him in his fight against evil.' This gift includes a clasp embossed with a jagged ray of lightning, 'given thee as a symbol of thy power' and which must be worn at his throat. Returned home in the space of a frame, Dave reads in the paper of a bank robbery. The gang is using a Paralizing (*sic*) Ray – 'This looks like a job for Litening!' Soon he is throwing the crooks every which way, including down the funnel of a ship. 'He's finished, and the ray with him. A fitting end for a madman!' And up in the clouds, Zeus and Mercury chuckle. 'It would seem that we have made a wise choice in this man!' 'Yea, he hath proved worthy of our trust!'

A rare attempt at a super-hero strip by Ron Embleton, a bright young artist who was more at home turning out western strips at the rate of one a week for Scion's series of *Big* comics. Embleton quickly evolved into one of England's finest strip cartoonists, producing wondrous colour work for *Express Weekly* (Wulf the Briton, 1957).

3D
BIG FLAME
WONDER COMIC
FEATURING LITENING
"LITENING" THE SON OF THE GODS
THE STORY OF A YOUNG MAN, WHO WAS FAVOURED BY THE GODS TO COMBAT THE FORCES OF EVIL.
AN OLD MAN STANDS IN A DESERTED STREET, WATCHING AND WAITING.
IN THAT SAME STREET A YOUNG MAN, DAVE TERRY, SAVES A CAT FROM THE JAWS OF A STRAY DOG.
RON
YOU ARE THE MAN I HAVE BEEN LOOKING FOR, A MAN WITH GOODNESS IN HIS HEART AND THE COURAGE TO PIT HIS STRENGTH AGAINST THE FORCES OF EVIL. COME, WE HAVE WORK TO DO.
IN A DAZE, DAVE FOLLOWS THE OLD MAN THROUGH CLOUDS OF SWIRLING VAPOUR TO THE HOME OF THE GODS WHERE HE IS GIVEN GREAT POWERS TO AID HIM IN HIS FIGHT AGAINST EVIL.

QUICKSILVER: THE WONDERMAN OF THE WEST
by William McCail
The Round Up (1948)
Children's Press (Glasgow)

Quicksilver the Wonderman was the first super-hero to have the 'green' touch, although printing methods meant he was clad in solid red! Described as 'protector of wild life', Quicksilver lived alone in a mountain cave, high above the prairie, whence he could keep an eagle eye open for devilry below. Thus when Coffin Reilly and his gang try to rope Shadow, the stallion leader of a wild herd of horses, Quicksilver dives down to the rescue, 'exerting his wonder powers to send the stallion up into an amazing leap which leaves Reilly's gang gasping with astonishment'. In revenge, Reilly sneaks into the secret cave and pumps six slugs into the sleeping super-hero. The bullets bounce off the body and Quicksilver takes the baddie for a flying 'ride'. The struggling gang boss falls from Quicksilver's grasp, straight into the path of the thundering herd. 'Justice has been done!' says the super-hero to the sky, 'I, Quicksilver, protector of the wild, am satisfied!'

Billy McCail's own independent commercial cartoon studio, Mallard Features, produced this comic-book for publication by the Glasgow-based Children's Press. The three-colour cover was drawn by Nat Brand.

The RoundUp

Budget of Fun and Adventure

"QUICKSILVER" Wonder Man of the West in a thrilling incident from the gripping yarn inside

ACE HART: THE ATOM MAN

by C. Purvis
Superthriller **No. 6 (1948)**
Foldes Press (Edinburgh)

'Ace Hart, a young scientist, has been able to harness atomic energy to his own body, which gives him the strength of twenty men, and enables him to fly faster than a jet.' Ace Hart's HQ is an extraordinary laboratory. When a crook kidnaps a judge's daughter with intent to hang her, Ace's screen lights up with the word 'Help!' Then 'the needle on Ace Hart's special receiver pinpoints the spot from where the cry came from' (*sic*). Remarks Ace, 'Two miles nor' west from Lulwich must be a hundred miles from here! I should be there in just a few minutes!' By the time he arrives, the killer is stringing the nightie-clad lovely to a tree-branch, crying 'Revenge is sweet! Ha-ha!' Ace arrives – 'Just in time, girlie!' – and hotly pursues the killer's aeroplane, grabbing its tail and turning it upside down. The killer falls out – *'Scream!'* – and Ace knocks him cold with a left swing, remarking, 'Bite on that one, sweetheart!' A second adventure in the same edition pitted Ace against Zonda, the glamour girl with hopes of ruling Britain. 'She is an expert in the art of hypnotism. With the aid of "The Eye", which flashed a powerful beam of light from long range into the victims' eyes, she could make them do her every wish!' explains Ace at some length.

C. Purvis not only drew Ace Hart, Atom Man, but also the back-up strips, Dick Daring and Tess Moran. Ace Hart was later taken over by James Bleach, and from issue No. 34 the comic was converted to *Western Super Thriller* in response to changing tastes among young readers. It finally closed after issue No. 82, an exceptionally long run.

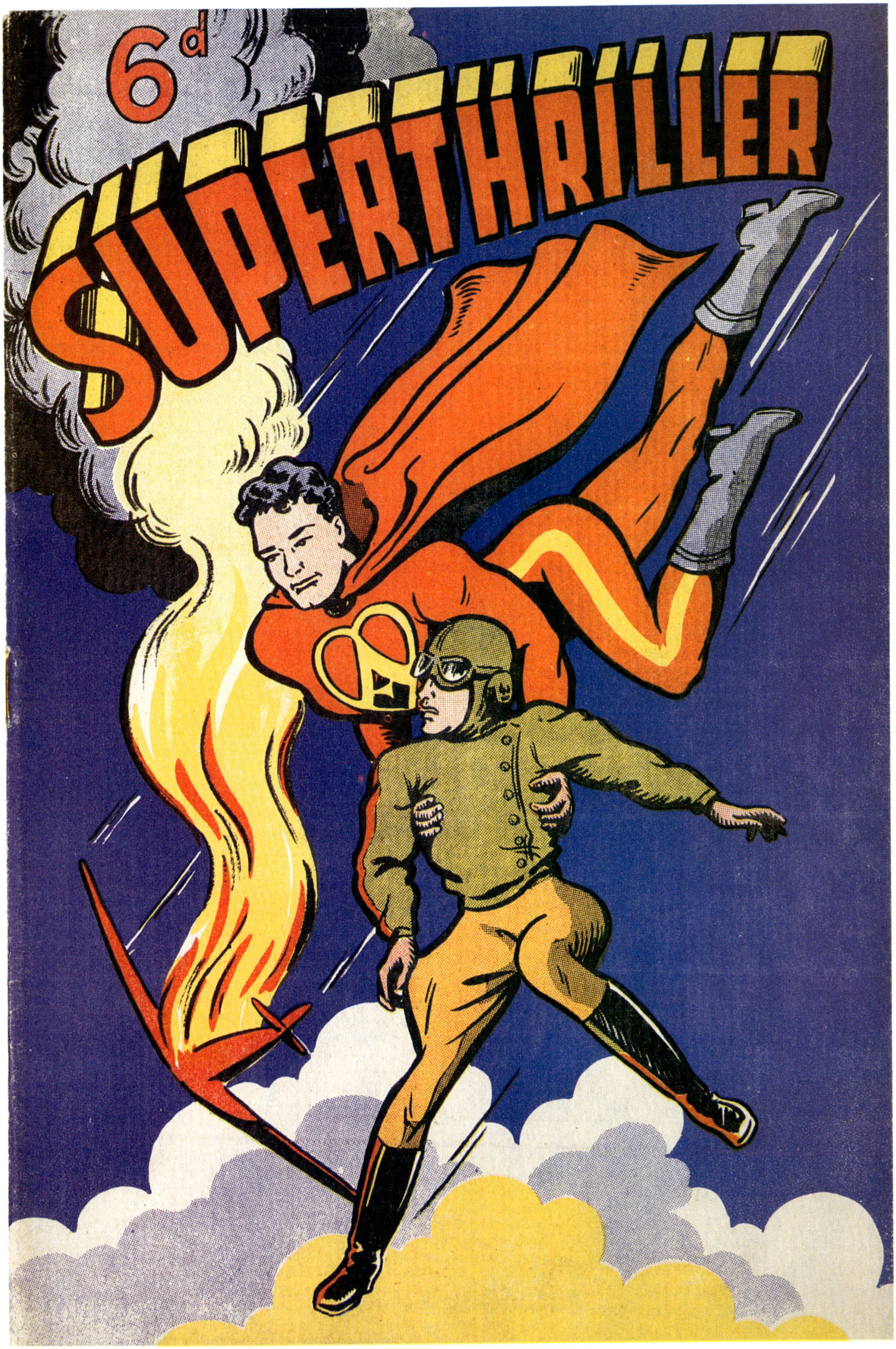
6d
SUPERTHRILLER

SUPER THRILLER ANNUAL

Ace Hart continued his adventures in the Christmas books, *Super Thriller Annual*. These were published in 1957, 1958 and 1959 by World Distributors of Manchester, who had taken over publication of the monthly comic-book in the mid-Fifties. Curiously, instead of being a book of strip cartoons, the Annual presented 128 pages of text stories. Thus Ace Hart played the lead in a series of stories which were illustrated, not by the artist for the comic-book, but by Edgar Hodges. It was Hodges who also painted the annual covers. Illustrated opposite is the third (1959) edition of the Annual, which featured Hart in the twelve-page story, 'Holiday in Space', written by Bryn Cullen. In this yarn Hart, described as 'the Superman who has the mysterious power of flight', works for Space Defence, and is accompanied by the glamourous Val.

It stretched out a hairy arm towards Val

THE SUPER THRILLER ANNUAL

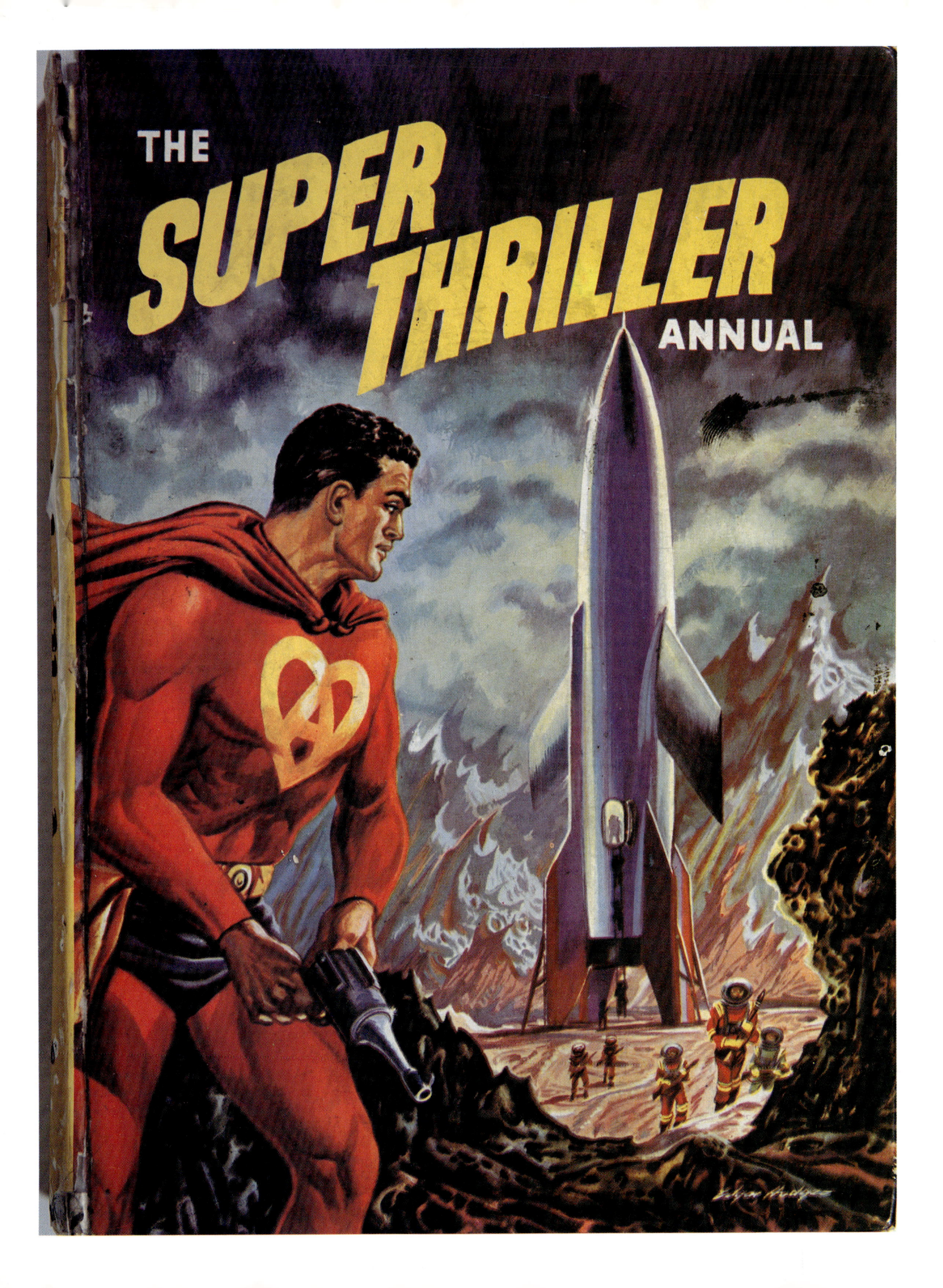

MASKMAN
**Big Game Comic (1948) Big Dynamo Comic (1948)
Scion Ltd (London)**

Maskman, who sported a black mask, a blue skin-tight suit, and a red letter 'M' on his chest, looked every inch a super-hero. In fact he was nothing of the sort, lacking any sort of super power save that, perhaps, of mystery. Maskman was the crime-busting alter ego of the Honourable Peter Pilkington, playboy, a secret known only to his faithful servant-cum-chauffeur, Fogg. This classy combo, the nearest comics ever got to the classic Wooster and Jeeves partnership, pottered about the fringes of crime among the upper crust with exclamations of 'By jove!', 'Bang-on!', and 'Oh, goody-goody, if I may say so, sir!' After a strenuous bout of noggin-boffing, the Hon. Maskman returned to his flat for a nightcap of port. 'Put this down past your tonsils, sir,' remarked Fogg.

Written and drawn by an unknown artist, Maskman appeared twice in the *Big* series of one-off comics published by Scion in the last years of paper restrictions, when new regular titles were still banned by wartime law.

THE BIG GAME COMIC presents MASKMAN

3D

THE HONOURABLE PETER PILKINGTON, OTHERWISE KNOWN AS "MASKMAN" TO HIS FAITHFUL SERVANT FOGG, IS ALARMED TO HEAR THAT HIS CAR HAS BEEN STOLEN, AND USED FOR A SMASH AND GRAB RAID! FOGG INFORMS PETER

BY JOVE! THE TRIPEHOUNDS HAVE THEY FOUND THE OLD BUS FOGG?

YES SIR AND THEY WANT YOU TO IDENTIFY IT.

OH RIGHTY HO!

SHE'S IN GOOD CONDITION SIR, OH! BANG NO DAMAGE DONE

OH! THANKS VERY MUCH CONSTABLE!

THAT'S THE FOURTH SMASH AND GRAB THIS WEEK! I ADVISE YOU TO KEEP YOUR CAR LOCKED IN FUTURE!

WE JOLLY WELL SHALL CONSTABLE. CHEERIO!

THEY ARRIVE AT THE POLICE STATION

FOGG OLD CHAP! I'VE A FEELING "MASKMAN" IS GOING TO APPEAR AGAIN, ONCE WE GET A CLUE ON THESE SMASH AND GRAB BOYS!

OH! GOODY! GOODY! IF I MAY SAY SO SIR!

HELLO!! WHAT'S THIS LYING ON THE FLOOR? FOGG! I THINK WE'VE GOT SOMETHING HERE!

REALLY SIR?

HO! HO! THE SMASH AND GRAB BOYS MUST HAVE DROPPED THIS IN THEIR HURRY! HMM, VERY INTERESTING, POLON ART SALON EH? FOGG, WE'RE GOING SALON SLUMMING!!

POLON ART SALON catalogue

PERCY FINDS A CLUE!

IT IS AN ART CATALOGUE

Published by Scion Ltd, and Printed by The Byron Press Ltd., Harrow.

CAPTAIN CRASH: DYNAMIC WONDER

by John McCail
Crash Comics **(1948)**
Rayburn Productions (London)

Headlined as 'The Dynamic Wonder', the editor of *Crash Comics* preferred the more euphonious 'Captain Crash the Thunderflash!' Perhaps this was because he was Bob Monkhouse, not yet a radio, TV and film star, but a fast-rising creator of comics. Crash had the cover plus a five-page lead feature in No. 1 of his own comic-book, a sixteen-page part-coloured sixpenny published by Martin & Reid under yet another of their pseudonyms. Alas, there was no No. 2. The foreword read, 'Captain Crash has power far beyond anything ever known. He can range space as he wills. Living in London as a young astronomer, he explored the heavens with his amazing telescope.' His is the first probe able to penetrate the reflective shield surrounding an unknown planet, where he observes the human crew of the space-liner Vulcan being treated as slaves by robots. Donning his crash-suit he zips through space at the speed of light, and crash-lands among a tribe of bird-like reptiles (or reptilian birds). The earthmen are slaves to the hypnotic power of Kling, Mad Ruler of Space, who is even now pulling another spaceship into his orbit. A quick grab of Kling's ray pistol soon blasts the Mad Ruler's head into shreds, and Crash's super-heroics are suitably rewarded: 'With the new power element, his own mighty power would be increased a thousand times!' Unfortunately we were never to be treated to the sight of such superness in action.

Created by veteran cartoonist John ('Jock') McCail, the first man to make an attempt at drawing the original Superman in a British comic. It was Jock who had drawn the two-colour covers of *Triumph* back in 1939, when that weekly introduced Siegel and Shuster's original character to an English audience. However, Jock's artwork never attained that cartoon-like quality demanded by American super-heroes, and he remained happier with horses in the many western strips he drew in his late years.

CRASH COMICS

No. 1 — 6d

featuring YARNS from the OLD NIGHT WATCHMAN SCREWLOOSE! CRACKERS! KRANKENSTEIN AND MANY OTHERS

CAPTAIN CRASH

VERSUS KLING — MAD RULER OF SPACE

WONDERMAN: THE ATOMIC MARVEL

by Mick Anglo
Wonderman (1948)
Paget Publications (London)

Also known as Captain Justice, Wonderman's adventures were invariably preceded by a printed foreword: 'John Justice, son of the world renowned scientist, the late Edward Justice, is a scientific product of his father's genius. Under the name of Captain Justice, John is known as an easy going, wealthy good-for-nothing, but secretly, in the guise of Wonderman, he uses his amazing strength, invulnerability, and superhuman atomic powers to fight evil.' From No. 2 of his monthly comic, the words 'and help humanity' were added. No explanation of his dead dad's experiments were ever given. Just the familiar-sounding phrase, 'This looks like a job for Wonderman!', and John's civvy suit vanished to be replaced by blue cloak, red and pink super-suit, and the emblazoned 'W' on the chest. This procedure, according to an explanatory balloon in No. 1, took one sixteenth of a second! Wonderman's powers were quite amazing in their casualness: to catch his first crooks he says, 'I'll have to travel back into time to witness the incident'. He sees the crime, 'I'm powerless to stop this foul act as it has already been done!', then nips forward again: 'Now to cast myself back into the present!' There are more abilities to be revealed. 'The blinds are drawn, but my X-ray eyes can see the crooks inside, and my super-radar ears can hear their conversation!' So it's through the wall, deflect the gunfire ('Bullets bounce from him!'), knock out four killers and deliver them to the local law with a wind-up homily: 'Nothing to it! Crime must never pay!'

First of many super-heroes created by Mick Anglo, Wonderman was the front page star of his own comic monthly, for which Anglo also created Nip McGee, Special Detective, and Trigger Lee, Texas Ranger. The comic was a success, running twenty-four issues and expanding from the standard threepenny eight-pager, to twelve pages from No. 8, to sixteen pages from No. 16. As Wonderman was wont to remark, 'Hot ziggety!'

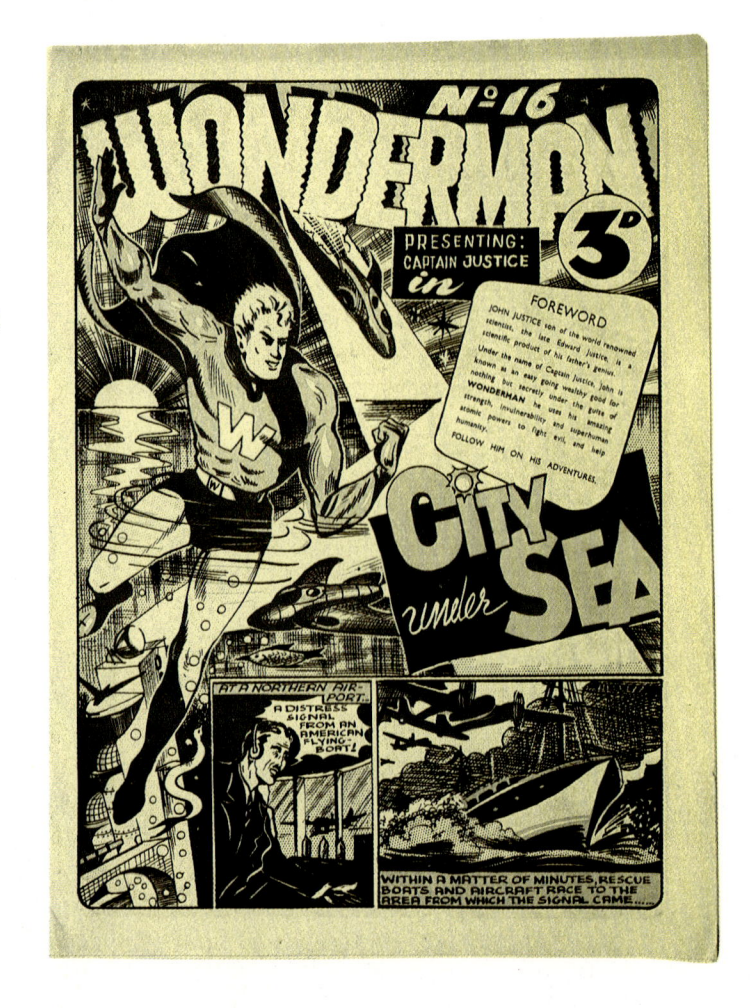

WONDERMAN
Presenting...
CAPTAIN JUSTICE ~ ATOMIC MARVEL
NIP McGEE ~ SPECIAL DETECTIVE
TRIGGER LEE ~ WESTERN
No. 4
price 3D.
FOREWORD
JOHN JUSTICE son of the world renowned scientist, the late Edward Justice, is a scientific product of his father's genius.
Under the name of Captain Justice, John is known as an easy going wealthy good for nothing but secretly under the guise of WONDERMAN he uses his amazing strength, invulnerability and superhuman atomic powers to fight evil, and help humanity.
FOLLOW HIM ON HIS ADVENTURES.
LISTEN TO ME JOHN JUSTICE. WHY DON'T YOU DO SOME USEFUL WORK INSTEAD OF LOAFING AROUND? YOU INFURIATE ME!
SOMETIMES I WISH I COULD TELL JAN I AM REALLY WONDERMAN BUT I GUESS IT'S BEST TO KEEP MY IDENTITY SECRET.
I'LL TAKE A CRUISE AROUND THE CITY AND SEE IF THERE IS ANYTHING THAT REQUIRES MY ATTENTION
WONDERMAN'S X-RAY VISION PIERCES THE ROADWAY.......
GOOD HEAVENS! SOMEBODY IS PLANTING A BOMB UNDERNEATH THE BANK!
THIS IS WHERE I TAKE A HAND
MICK

THE TORNADO
by Bob Monkhouse
Oh Boy! Comics (1948)
Paget Publications (London)

Steve Storm, ace reporter on the *London Tribune*, is a man with a strange secret. 'To reveal the secret of this, the thirteenth member of the notorious Storm family, we take you back to the 15th century. Under the leadership of a courageous young lawyer, Stephen Storm, honest citizens of the monastery village of Monkhouse (*tee-hee!*) seize the wicked leader of the monks! They are merely a band of murderers and thieves, and as Grosta, the chief villain, is led to the gallows, he utters a passionate curse: 'Stephen Storm, by all the black lords of evil, I here condemn the men of the Storm line to lives of crime and cruelty, unto the limits of my power – five hundred years!' Well, to cut an extremely long preamble short, 500 years later: 'Like the bursting pressure of the Perra Volcano, the mighty force of the Storms thundered into the soul of Steve Storm, that this powerful young hero might, at will, transform himself to the giant superman of justice, whirlwind prince of the storms – Tornado!' Soon action begins, delayed only by the cartoonist's verbiage. At the exploding volcano of Perra, 'the great bubbling hills of decayed vegetation begin to shift. Strangely, slowly, a mass of the stinking glutinous fungi and foul mud, disgorged by the great eruption, swells and belches up out of the gaseous lake. Heaving and twisting it moulds itself into a monstrous shape, dragging its steaming bulk up from the sea of sulphurous lava!' As the animated heap hobbles onward it swallows everything in its path, growing bigger with every gulp. 'This looks like a job for Tornado!' shouts Steve. 'In a flash Steve, by a concentrated effort of his mighty will, becomes Tornado!' After trying punches, water and fire, Tornado comes up with the perfect Growth Destroyer: weedkiller!

Bob Monkhouse is undoubtedly the best comics talent ever lost to showbiz. Art apart, his excellent wordplay reaches heights hitherto unknown in British comics, while at times his illustrations show a sexuality that quite defeated Paget Publications' editorial censor. Later artists on Tornado included Ron Embleton.

NUMBER TWO THE TORNADO IN

OH BOY! COMICS

THE PUNCH PACKED PAPER ★ OF THRILLS AND FUN!

TORNADO ON THE ATOM PLANET 3D

NO! THIS IS NOT JUST ONE OF THOSE "PLANET" STORIES —

SOMETHING FAR STRANGER THAN A BUNCH OF WHIRLING ROCKETS AND HURTLING STRATOPLANES HAS HAPPENED, BEFORE WE FIND THE MIGHTY TORNADO JUST WAKING UP IN WEIRD SURROUNDINGS! LET'S START AT THE BEGINNING

STORY AND ART BY Ramon

MR. STEVE STORM? I AM PROFESSOR WYATT, BACTERIOLOGIST AND MICRO-SPECIALIST! I NEED YOUR HELP DESPERATELY, MR. STORM, TO RESCUE MY DAUGHTER, GLORIA, FROM WHAT MAY WELL BE A LIVING DEATH!

HOW CAN I HELP, PROFESSOR?

ATOM: THE MIGHTY BOY
The Rocket Comic (1948)
P.M. Productions (London)

It is the year 2000 AD, today around the corner, but when No. 1 of *The Rocket* was published, over half a century away. The world is in sudden peril: 'Mighty tempests and terrific tidal waves have ravaged many lands; huge liners have been attacked and dragged down by gigantic brutes from the sea-bed. Other marine monsters raid coastal cities, and civilisation is threatened. Terrified scientists finally decide that a hitherto-unknown race in the depths of the ocean is out to conquer and destroy mankind!' Then, to the rescue of the world, comes Atom the Mighty Boy, and Elektra his Fearless Sister! Diving from a spaceship into a mighty maelstrom, the fearnoughts fight fearsome fish-men while their heel-rockets shoot them through a giant tunnel in the sea-bed. Braving a blazing wall of fire, they plunge down into a vast crater. Instantly they are set upon by grotesque sea-beasts, 'half-man, half-brute, but intelligent and disciplined'. Elektra is quickly caught, but Atom 'uses his blazing iridium sword that destroys all it touches'. Saving his sister, Atom fails to check the sea-beasts with a handful of atom-pellets. The pair's last card is to bombard the thin rock walls of the crater with their ray guns. Steam fills the lair, acting as poison gas to the sea-beasts. 'With their fearful enemies doomed en masse, Atom and Elektra retreat in triumph to the surface of the sea.' They receive the thanks of a world restored to peace – until Bird-men from Space attack the world in *Rocket Comic* No. 2!

Rocket was one of the many first-class comic-books published by Philipp Marx. These were edited by ex-Amalgamated Press men, who knew a good comic artist when they saw one, and understood the young minds of their readers. Marx comics were a successful mixture of traditional style, quality and a modern approach to design and characterisation, without emulating what were then known as 'Americanisms'.

ATOM - THE MIGHTY BOY
V
THE BIRD-MEN
ROCKET
4D
COMIC No. TWO
A.D. 2000. ASTRONOMERS LEARN THAT NEWLY-DISCOVERED BIRD-MEN FROM SPACE ARE ABOUT TO ATTACK THE WORLD. AGAIN, ATOM, THE MIGHTY BOY, AND ELEKTRA, HIS SISTER, FLY TO THE RESCUE!
CONT. ON BACK PAGE.

RAY SPEDE: THE ROCKET MAN
by C. Montford
Red Flash Comic **(1948)** *Bob Comic Book* **(1949)**
Philmar Ltd (London)

Ray Spede was the two-colour front and back page star of this fourpenny comic-book. A flying man, a familiar comic strip hero since the days of Clem Sohn, the Thirties pioneer, Ray Spede was described as a scientist-adventurer, while his winged apparatus was dubbed 'his new rocket-ornithopter'. Out testing one night, Ray is nearly mown down by a mysterious plane. Suddenly he spots a figure falling from the plane. 'Like a winged streak he dives to the rescue!' He catches her as she is about to crash onto a passing car, and learns she is Joan St Clair, 'daughter of the famous millionaire'. She and her small brother were kidnapped by the Flight Gang, to be held to ransom. 'Using the full power of his rockets, Ray hits the sky-trail after the gang.' Overhauling the crooks' plane he shadows them through moonlight to a secret airfield where, 'like an angry hawk, he swoops to save the boy from the ruthless gang!' Then he wings away to new adventures, in No. 2 of *Red Flash Comic* – where much to his surprise he found himself drawn by a different artist, Colin Merritt!

C. Montford was one of the sturdier talents of the pre-war Amalgamated Press, so it is no surprise to find him working for one of Philipp Marx's comic companies where AP editors and artists found a busy haven in the days of paper rationing. Montford, known for such movie star western strips as 'Bob Baker' and 'Roy Rogers' in *The Wonder*, seemed to be adept at any kind of adventure strip. Colin Merritt took over in *Bob Comic Book*. He was another pre-war AP adventure artist and had drawn 'Chums of the E-Men Patrol' for *Chips* (1937).

BOB COMIC BOOK

28 PACKED PAGES!

1/-

RAY SPEDE IN THE UNDERWORLD OF PTUR

THE LENNOX EXPEDITION HAS JOURNEYED TO AMAZONIA TO EXPLORE THE VAST DEPTHS OF THE EXTINCT VOLCANO, PTUR. NO TRANSPORT CAN TACKLE THE SHEER WALLS OF THE CRATER, WHICH REACH DOWN TO UNPLUMBED DEPTHS: AND OWING TO DENSE JUNGLE MASSED IN THE CRATER, NO AIRPLANE ATTEMPT CAN BE MADE. THEREFORE PROFESSOR LENNOX HAS DESIGNED AN ORNITHOPTER — MECHANICAL BIRD WINGS EQUIPPED WITH PHOTOGRAPHIC AND RADIO APPARATUS. RAY SPEDE, FAMOUS FREE-LANCE ADVENTURER, IS THE THRILL-SEEKER WHO VOLUNTEERS TO FLY DOWN ALONE INTO THE UNCHARTED UNKNOWN......

(CONT. ON BACK PAGE)

GAIL GARRITY: GIRL WONDER

by Mick Anglo
Dynamic (1949) *Oh Boy! Comics* (1949)
Paget Publications (London)

'Look Out for Gail Garrity!' was the regular catchline to this super-gal's knockout adventures, which started on the front page of *Dynamic*, a one-shot sixpenny special put out by Paget Publications in February 1949. Afterwards she became a regular in *Oh Boy! Comics* from No. 8. Like Wonderman, Gail had her own regular printed foreword, which read: 'Gail Garrity, daughter of Buck Garrity, the noted scientist, big-game hunter and soldier of fortune, has been trained since early childhood to face all sorts of danger. In addition to being a clever scientist and linguist, Gail is an expert in judo and swordsmanship, is a crack shot and an ace pilot. As a reporter on the National Tribune, Gail is able to use her unusual gifts in a remorseless fight against crime.' Apart from wondering whether 'swordsmanship' might not better read 'swordsgirlship', Gail was obviously striking an early blow for fighting feminism, especially as comics entitled *Dynamic* and *Oh Boy* clearly have a built-in boy appeal. Gail's first four-page assignment, an interview with the notorious Killer Miller, displayed plenty of action, fisticuffs and leg, rarely seen in British comics of the Forties. Although she never sported a super-costume, Gail was quite super enough for most readers of threepenny comics.

Mick Anglo's only heroine, Gail Garrity was closer to Buck Ryan's glamorous helpmate, Zola, than to Norman Pett's popular strip girl, Jane. A pioneer of fighting gals in British comics, Gail was clearly inspired by the 'good girl' art that was currently coming from American comic-book publishers. Gail's adventures were later taken over by Jack Bridges.

YOU'LL BE AHEAD WITH DYNAMIC

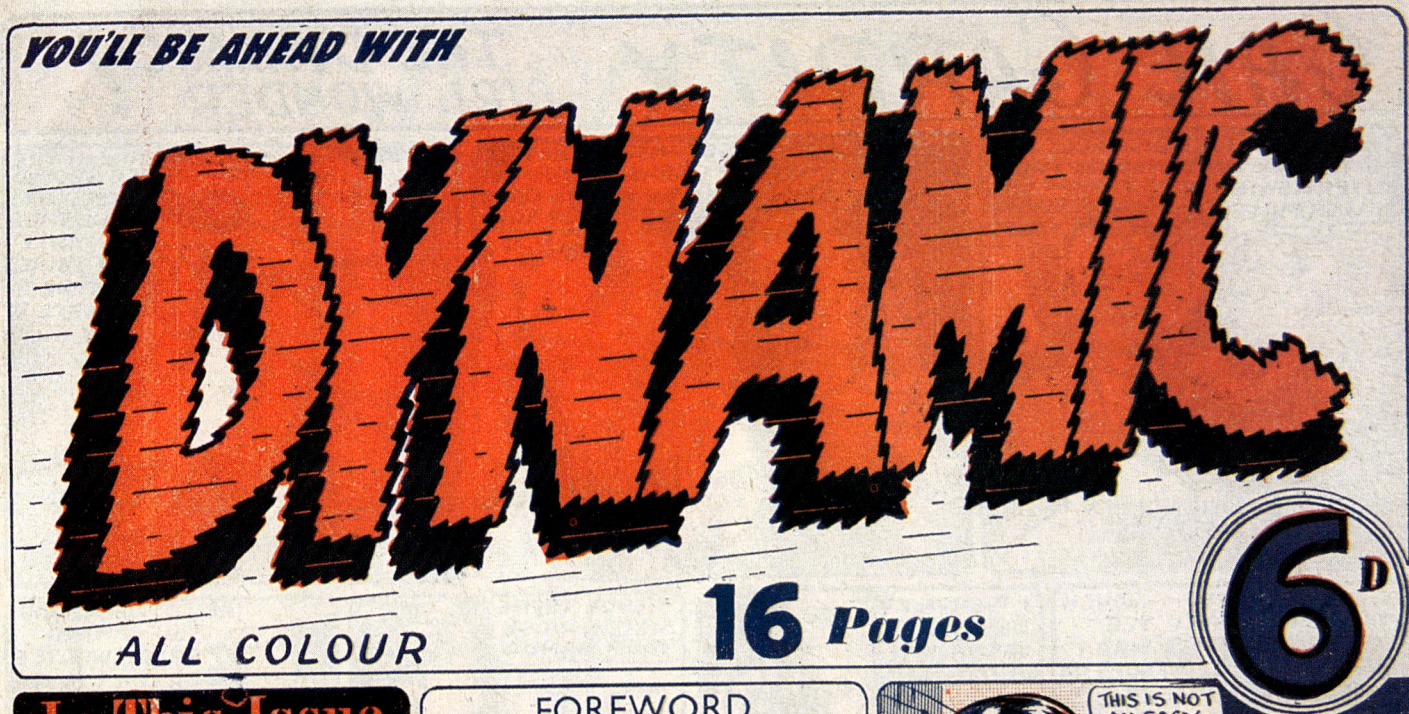

ALL COLOUR — **16 Pages** — **6D**

In This Issue
- GAIL GARRITY GIRL WONDER
- WONDERMAN (BY SPECIAL ARRANGEMENT WITH WONDERMAN COMICS)
- ALSO CYCLONE – U.N.O. INVESTIGATOR
- JACK FENTON – F.O. AGENT
- STUPORMAN & OTHER FEATURES

FOREWORD

GAIL GARRITY, daughter of BUCK GARRITY, the noted scientist, big-game hunter and soldier of fortune, has been trained since early childhood to face all sorts of danger.

In addition to being a clever scientist and linguist, Gail is an expert in Judo and swordsmanship, is a crack shot and an ace pilot.

As a reporter on the "National Tribune," Gail is able to use her unusual gifts in a remorseless fight against crime.

LOOK OUT FOR GAIL GARRITY.

"THIS IS NOT AN EASY ASSIGNMENT GAIL BUT I KNOW I CAN DEPEND ON YOU"

"DON'T WORRY E.Q. I'LL TAKE CARE OF IT"

"I'LL SAY IT'S NOT AN EASY ASSIGNMENT. KILLER MILLER DOESN'T LIKE GIVING INTERVIEWS TO THE PRESS"

"IT WON'T TAKE ME LONG TO DRIVE OUT TO KILLER'S COUNTRY HOUSE BUT GETTING IN TO SEE HIM IS ANOTHER MATTER"

"WELL, THERE'S THE PLACE — HERE GOES!"

"HEY THERE SISTER! NOT SO FAST, I WANT A WORD WITH YOU"

"O.K. SISTER, JUST TAKE IT EASY. WHAT ARE YOU DOING SNOOPING AROUND HERE?"

"HASN'T ANYBODY EVER TOLD YOU IT'S RUDE TO POINT A GUN AT A LADY"

OW!

CAPTAIN MIGHT: THE NEMESIS OF CRIME!
By Denis Gifford
Amazing Comics (1949)
Modern Fiction Ltd (London)

'Meet Professor Alan English, research scientist at Atomville, secret village of atomic workers somewhere in England.' A quick scene set and 'Hallo!' says Prof English, 'these solutions are reacting strangely – I wonder why? Perhaps if I...' A blinding flash strikes the prof in mid-sentence. 'Phew!' says the prof, 'that's odd! I feel amazing strength surging through me! Must be due to atomic radiation! I'm a superman – and that gives me an idea! I'll outdo those comic-book heroes – as Captain Might!' Within one frame he is clad in a star-emblazoned super-suit, seeking a way to use his new powers to fight crime. (Interesting that a professor of atomic science should be thoroughly familiar with comics and their conventions.) That night in Atomville's own theatre, Alan finds a way when Marvo the Magician waves his wand and vanishes none other than Prof Maxted, the big chief: 'And now I am going to vanish, too! Farewell, fools!' And the magician disappears in a puff of smoke. Soon Captain Might is on the trail via a dropped visiting card to Black Retreat, where he saves the stripped chief from Marvo's red-hot poker. 'Wherever there is a wrong to be righted, there you will find Captain Might!' But you will have to search hard – he never appeared again!

Captain Might was the star of *Amazing Comics*, one of several one-shot titles I produced for Modern Fiction Ltd. These included *Funtown*, *Hooray* and *Modern Comics*, which latter may be found in our companion volume *Space Aces!*

THE WORLD OF TODAY MEETS THE WORLD OF TOMORROW IN...
COLOUR
FICTION
AMAZING
COMICS
3D.
INTRODUCING
THE NEMESIS OF CRIME!
CAPTAIN MIGHT
BY DENIS GIFFORD CREATOR OF TIGERMAN AND Streamline
HALLO – THESE SOLUTIONS ARE REACTING STRANGELY – I WONDER WHY? PERHAPS IF I —
MEET PROFESSOR ALAN ENGLISH, RESEARCH SCIENTIST AT ATOMVILLE, SECRET VILLAGE OF ATOMIC WORKERS, SOMEWHERE IN ENGLAND.
SUDDENLY – A BLINDING FLASH!
PHEW! THAT'S ODD – I FEEL AMAZING STRENGTH SURGING THROUGH ME – MUST BE DUE TO THE ATOMIC RADIATION! I'M A SUPER-MAN – AND THAT GIVES ME AN IDEA – I'LL OUTDO THOSE COMICBOOK HEROES!
– AS CAPTAIN MIGHT!
HOPE I GET A CHANCE TO USE MY POWERS TO FIGHT CRIME SOON – IT'S BEEN FOUR DAYS NOW –
FOR FOUR DAYS ALAN TESTS HIS STRENGTH, GETTING CONTROL OVER HIS NEW POWERS – WAITING, WAITING...
IT'S SWELL THE WAY THE ATOMVILLE AUTHORITIES PROVIDE FIRST CLASS ENTERTAINERS FOR US ATOM WORKERS!
MARIO THE MAGICIAN, EH? HAVEN'T SEEN HIM SINCE PRE-WAR!
THE NEXT NIGHT, ALAN VISITS ATOMVILLE'S OWN THEATRE –
HAVING MADE THE DOVES DISAPPEAR, I SHOULD LIKE THE ASSISTANCE OF A MEMBER OF THE AUDIENCE IN MY NEXT TRICK – PERHAPS YOU WILL OBLIGE, SIR?
WHO-ME? SURELY – I'D BE GLAD TO!
THAT'S PROF. MAXTED – THE BIG CHIEF!
PRESTO!
A WAVE OF THE WAND – AND THE PROFESSOR VANISHES!
HA! HA! OLD MAXTED'S GONE!
– AND NOW I AM GOING TO VANISH TOO! FAREWELL, YOU FOOLS!
GOOD LORD! IS THIS PART OF THE SHOW – OR – WHAT?
?
CONTINUED ON PAGE 4

CAPTAIN MAGNET
by Crewe Davies
Super Duper Comics (1949)
Cartoon Art Productions (Glasgow)

'My name is Velvet McCall,' she said in a big closeup. 'I'm here to tell you everything I know of Johnny Calhoon and Captain Magnet, the guy who keeps one jump ahead of the spin of a revolver chamber… the guy who gives crookdom never-ending strikes at their apparent security.' She starts her story in Detroit, capital of Michigan, in an office of the OSS at a time near the end of World War Two. It seems a non-Nazi Kraut, name of Schrag, has discovered 'some ginkazoo that's reputed to bust every known paragraph of the mystic law of gravity.' 'Imagine what the swastika army could do with that little brain-child!' says Johnny's boss. Before the second page ends, Calhoon is bailing out over Angermunde where he is made very welcome by Velvet McCall, no less. Three pages later the war is over, and Johnny is swallowing the secret formula and changing into Captain Magnet, costumed ready to combat the post-war evils.

Created by prolific designer of Anglo-American super-heroes, Dennis M. Reader, Captain Magnet was continued after his initial adventure by Crewe Davies, whose artwork was more finished if his dialogue was less breezy.

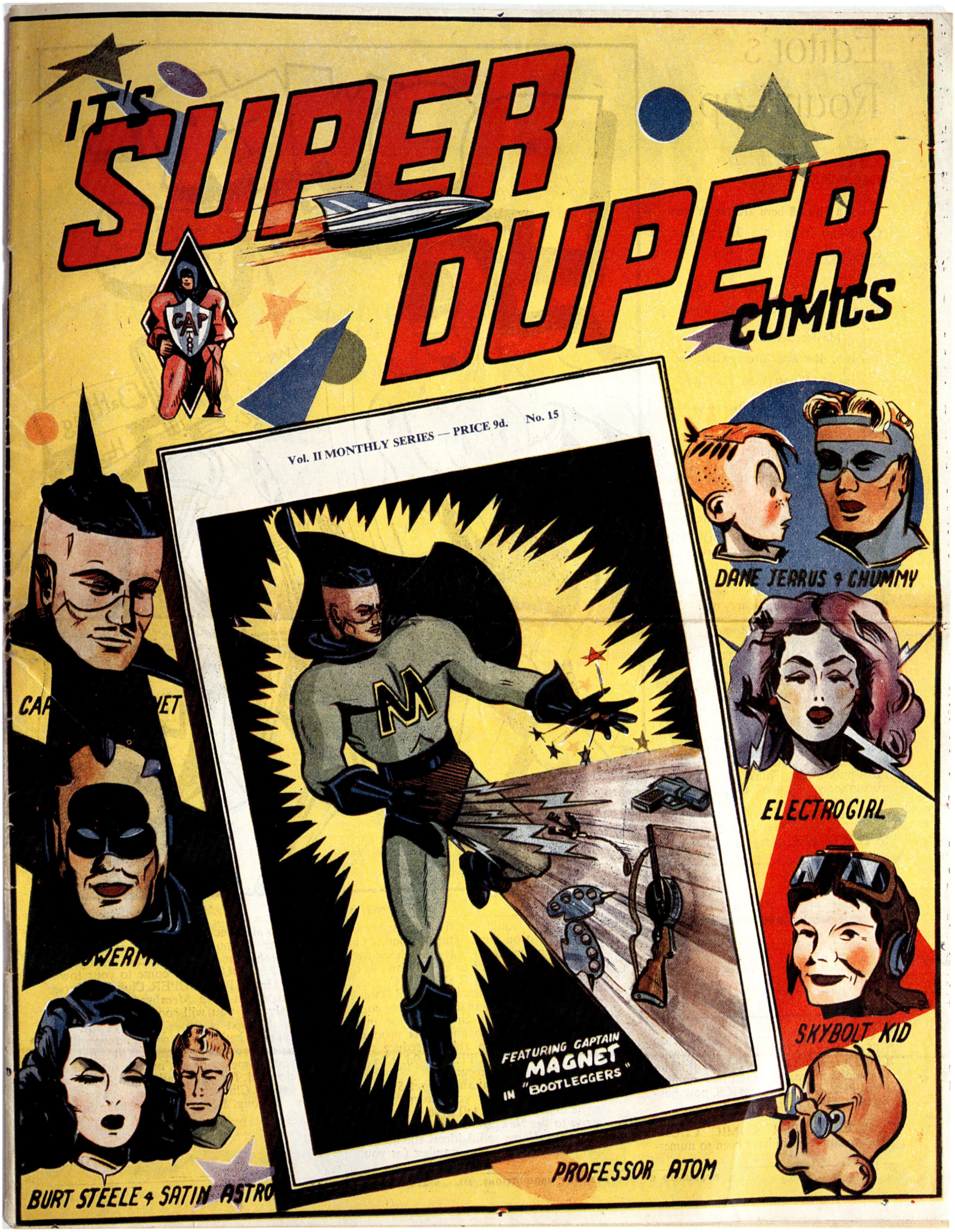
IT'S SUPER DUPER COMICS
CAP
Vol. II MONTHLY SERIES — PRICE 9d. No. 15
FEATURING CAPTAIN MAGNET IN "BOOTLEGGERS"
DANE JERRUS & CHUMMY
ELECTROGIRL
SKYBOLT KID
PROFESSOR ATOM
BURT STEELE & SATIN ASTRO

CAPTAIN ZENITH

by Mick Anglo
Captain Zenith Comic **(1950)**
Martin & Reid Ltd (London)

Captain Zentih, clad in a red skin-tight outfit and helmet, and emblazoned both front and back with a large letter 'Z', arrived rather late in the super-hero field, despite being described in a caption as 'the amazing man of speed'. But by 1950 there was no need to explain a super-hero, so no time was wasted in showing how he came to be. The description 'Upholder of Justice' was enough, the word 'Help!' in a stray speech-balloon being sufficient to send Captain Zenith leaping into action. Speed may be Zenith's watchword, but it is also his handicap, for he loses the car he is pursuing – 'I've been too fast!' he says. But not so, for it is all a crook's trick. 'Take that, you crooks!' cries the Captain, delivering a sock or so, plus the usual end-picture homily: 'One way or another, the Law Always Wins!'

One of artist Mick Anglo's less successful creations, Captain Zenith made but one appearance. At least he was starred in his own title. This 'Mascot Comic' was published by one of the most prolific small publishers of the period, Martin & Reid of Bishopsgate.

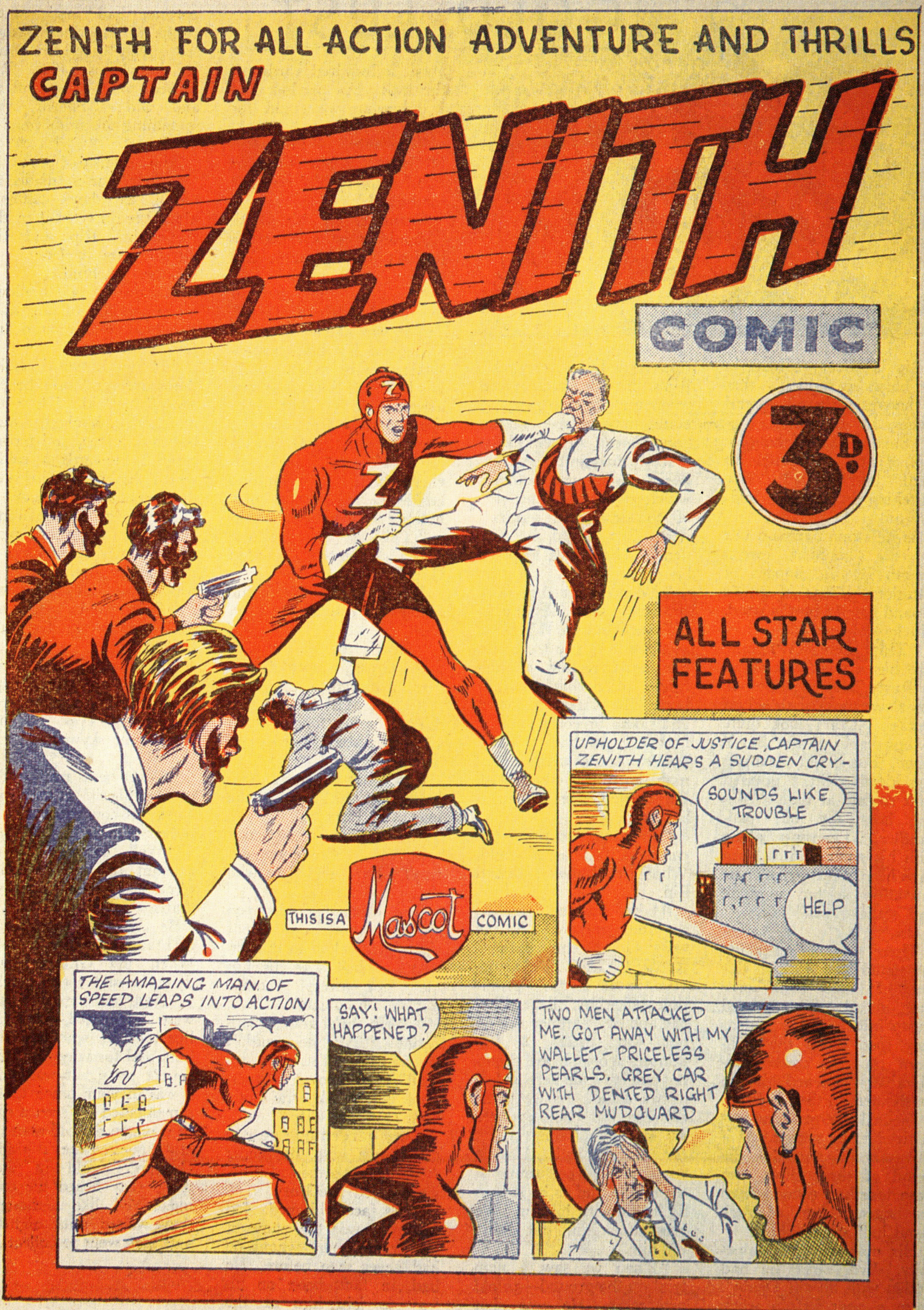

Continued on back page

ELECTROMAN
by King-Ganteaume Productions
Electroman Comics **(1951)** *In Orbit* **(c. 1955)**
Scion Ltd (London) George Turton (London)

In an adventure entitled 'The Birth of Electroman', the amazing story is told of 'kind, elderly, New York City newsboy Dan Watkins, who was once an arch-criminal, but because of a strange and amazing fate, has renounced his former life of crime and has become a staunch ally for the forces of law and order in their unending battle to stamp out evil!' It seems Dan, once known throughout the criminal trade as Fingers, was sent to the electric chair for a murder he did not commit. Amazingly, despite 200,000 volts of current shot through him, he survives. More, as the prison doc states, 'Warden, the shock has cured the mental disease which in his case made this man a criminal!' Pronounced legally dead, the now bald Fingers is released, and proceeds to track down the real killer. Caught by the evil Baron Kotzbue, Dan is tied to a high voltage electric cable and given a fatal shot of juice. But with a *'Z-Z-Z-Z-POW!'*, 'the second powerful shockwave in some strange way altered the molecular structure of my ordinary body and I became Electroman, with superhuman power to defeat the forces of evil!' Complete with cape, boots and a crossed lightning-flash emblem, Electroman rounds up the crooks with a cry of 'Better say your prayers, you punks!' while they stand open-mouthed in surprise saying things like 'Hey, the bullets just bounce off him!' Afterwards, how does Dan change back? Easy – 'By merely grounding my electronic power!' And when Electroman is needed to answer the call to crush crime? 'All I need do is touch a live wire or switch!' As tiny Tim the would-be crook remarked, 'Gee! Gosh! Crime sure doesn't pay!'

Electroman was one of a series of comic-books packaged for publishers by the specialist agency, King-Ganteaume Productions, a studio said to have been set up on their severance gratuity by two former GIs. Certainly, their story-lines and dialogue teemed with authentic American comic-book slang.

ELECTROMAN
COMICS
WHAM!
BANG!
BANG!
BANG!
BANG!
A SCION COMIC
6D
U.K. EDITION
KING-GANTEAUME PROD.

MR APOLLO
by George Bunting
Dynamic Thrills (1952)
Gerald G. Swan Ltd (London)

Jerry Gunn is a bespectacled, pipe-puffing school-teacher with a secret. He is also Mr Apollo, 'a super-human with the Strength of Hercules, plus the Speed of Mercury!' As these are two of the talents that go to make up the magic word 'Shazam!', which changes Billy Batson into Captain Marvel, it is perhaps small wonder that Jerry Gunn's other half looks remarkably like that American super-hero, right down to the doubled-folded cloak. His chest emblem is different, however, being a star with a tail (not, we hasten to add, the old gag – Lassie!). Mr Apollo appears on the scene by some instant physical change wrought by Jerry's mind. 'In an instant the humble Jerry Gunn becomes Mr Apollo, the man whom no bonds can hold!' This enables him to thwart such evil creatures as Varda the Human Bat, Karlas the Hunter of Humans, and a trio of monsters released from an ancient Tibetan casket. Oddest of his opponents was undoubtedly Toby, the fat schoolboy who swallowed some of Professor Calitrope's atomic pills and expanded into a fat giant!

Mr Apollo's debut in *Dynamic Thrills* was heralded by the special cover drawn by John McCail. This comic-book was the last in Gerald G. Swan's prolific series of titles, which had begun in January 1940 with *New Funnies*. A thirty-six-page black-and-white comic-book for sixpence, McCail made the mistake of including the word 'coloured' on the cover, which had to be blotted out, rather spoiling the balance of the lettering. Mr Apollo also appeared in *Slick Fun Album* (1952), *Cute Fun Album* (1953) and *Funnies Album* (1953).

DYNAMIC THRILLS

No. 7

MR APOLLO SMASHES THROUGH

6ᴅ

36 PICTURE PAGES

MASTERMAN
by Joe Colquhoun
Masterman Comic (1952)
United Anglo-American Book Co / Streamline (London)

In Longvale, California, lives bespectacled Bobby Fletcher, looking remarkably like an English schoolboy in his short trousers and neat haircut. Bobby, however, has a secret, which he explains in a 'thinks' balloon: 'Little does he know that I can transform myself into the mighty Masterman by rubbing my Ring of Fate, and saying "O Ring of Fate, I call upon you to help me fight for freedom and justice!" ' Meanwhile his dad and his teacher are discussing the end of the world as we know it. It seems the polar ice cap is getting too heavy and likely to shift the Earth's axis, 'causing a disruption of the entire land and water distribution, and completely destroy our civilisation!' Bobby's dad, being an oil magnate, persuades Congress to use the atom bomb, not realising that the whole thing is a plot by Master Spy Azzovsky, minion of the Dictator of Demonacia, to make the West use up its atom bombs and clear the way for demonic invasion. Fortunately a rub of his Ring of Fate and *'Pow!'* – Masterman, complete in eagle insignia and skirt (well, perhaps kilt might be a kinder word), erupts in time to kayo the Demonacians by throwing their atom-bombers into one another before they can wipe out the West!

Masterman achieved a goodly run of twelve monthly editions before succumbing to another comic-book craze and changing its title to *Masterman Western*. Several of Masterman's well-drawn if wordy adventures were printed in full colour, a rare experience for a British super-

MASTERMAN
COMIC
6d
NOVEMBER 1952
POW!
STREAMLINE
AMERICAN COMIC
VOS IS DIS, MAGIC?
KING-GANTEAUME PROD.

CAPTAIN VIGOUR: STRONGMAN OF SPORT

by Philip Mendoza
Captain Vigour (1952) *Steve Samson* (1953)
Sports Cartoons Ltd (Surbiton)

What Captain Vigour lacked in a Christian name he made up for with his moustache, the only super-hero to be so adorned. Nor did he wear a uniform, only his everyday safari suit and solar topee. For Vigour was a self-made strong man, and ex-Olympic champion. Now retired, he was a member of the Central Committee of the Olympic Games, searching Britain and the Commonwealth for athletic talent. In his first appearance, Vigour is bound for West Africa and Labadi village, where lives a boy who, reports a Dr Mackie, can run 100 yards in 8.9 seconds. 'It sounds impossible!' says Vigour, and indeed it now is for the boy, Lahai, lies in a coma, paralysed by a ju-ju spell cast by Witch Doctor Levuma. The adventure grows more exciting by the panel as the jungle is set alight, Vigour tries a spot of hand-to-jaw fighting with a giant crocodile, and finally defeats a whole herd of the Witch Doctor's prehistoric dragons! In later adventures a clean-shaven Captain found himself Chief of the Interplanetary Security Police Investigation Bureau, assisted by young Skeets Ryan.

Veteran artist Philip Mendoza, who drew everything from comics to sexy paperback covers for Hank Janson novels, had no truck with the usual super-hero fantasy in his treatment of Captain Vigour. The basic idea was to present to boys a hero they could actually emulate, especially if they sent half-a-crown (12½ pence) to the Body Sculpture Club: 'Muscles like Granite! But Flexible as Whalebone! Five Pulsating Courses by the Champion of Champions, George F. Jowett!'

MONTHLY PUBLICATION
Nº 1
Captain VIGOUR
STRONGMAN OF SPORT
BRITISH APPROVED COMIC
6D.
"AFRICAN JOURNEY"

STEVE SAMSON: STRONG MAN OF THE CIRCUS

by Nat Brand
Steve Samson **(1953)**
Sports Cartoons Ltd (Surbiton)

'Ladeez and gentlemen!' cries the ringmaster. 'Meet Steve Samson, the mighty man, the steel-muscled giant of the ring!' Not the boxing ring, but the sawdust ring of Major Lambert's International Circus, giving its first comic-book performance in the town of Gretville. Samson, a blond Tarzan type in loincloth looking remarkably like the same artist's previous creation, Halcon, Lord of the Crater-Land, brings the crowd to its feet with a dynamic display of super strength: he lifts twelve grown men on a plank balanced on his head! Then he catches Ron the aerialist when his trapeze is sabotaged by a rival showman, Green of the Motor Maniacs. The circus is set ablaze and King the killer lion is loosed, two simple tasks for the Strong Man of the Circus, even if twenty-four pages of pictures must pass before the feud concludes. Then Colonel Lovatt of MI5 comes calling, and next issue Steve is working in the jungles of Loolang as a secret agent!

Steve Samson's monthly comic-book was the most successful of the several titles published by Sports Cartoons Ltd, who had the indignity of being misspelled Sport Carton in their first issue! Several artists worked on the series, which ran to forty issues, with a weekly publication schedule from No. 18. The best was undoubtedly James Holdaway, destined to rise fast and die young. Unfortunately he drew only the covers from No. 3 to No. 11. Fantasy entered Steve's scenario with No. 12, when he joined the first space rocket crew and flew to Mars. Stranger still was the next episode, which opened with Steve summoned before the Elders of the Universe in their Chamber of Eternal Wisdom, where he was presented with the anti-gravity Seal of the Gods!

MONTHLY PUBLICATION
STEVE
SAMSON
JAWS of DEATH
BRITISH
SPORTS
CARTOONS
COMIC

SUPERSTOOGE

by Harry Banger
Slick Fun Album **(1953, 1956)** *Funnies Album* **(1953)**
Gerald G. Swan Ltd (London)

Stoogie, a classic comic-strip simpleton with his big nose, big eyes, big head and big bowler hat, suffered the longest life of any of Harry Banger's many heroes for the Gerald G. Swan comic-books. Born in No. 1 of *Topical Funnies* (April 1940), Stoogie suffered through a slapstick series of double-page misadventures, achieving such popularity that he was eventually promoted to front page star of *Coloured Slick Fun*, Swan's only weekly. After a decade of disasters, Stoogie finally achieved some kind of revenge by blossoming into a super-hero, of all things! As Banger's foreword put it, 'Endowed with superhuman powers, our old friend Stoogie has ample opportunities to make up for his previous humdrum existence – and how!' It all began with a strange encounter of the kind kind: he carried an old codger's bundle home and was suitably rewarded with a glass of peculiar pop. With a gasp of 'Phaff! Ug!' Stoogie was changed into a cloaked and S-emblazoned superchap. 'Go forth and do all the good deeds you wish!' said the bearded old boy. But things still went wrong for Stoogie – he unzipped a raincloud to help a dried-out farmer, but swamped his land with the drenching downpour!

Burlesque versions of Superman and his mighty ilk had long been a popular subgenre in American comic-books. The first British satirical super-hero was Stuporman, billed variously as the Atomic Comic, the Musclebound Moron, the Champion Chump and the Addlepated Atlas. Created by Bob Monkhouse, he backed up The Tornado in *Oh Boy! Comics* (1948). The American craze finally caught up with that very traditional British cartoonist, Harry Banger, in 1953, although he had been drawing Tornado Tom, a terribly tough cowboy, since the Forties.

SLICK FUN ALBUM

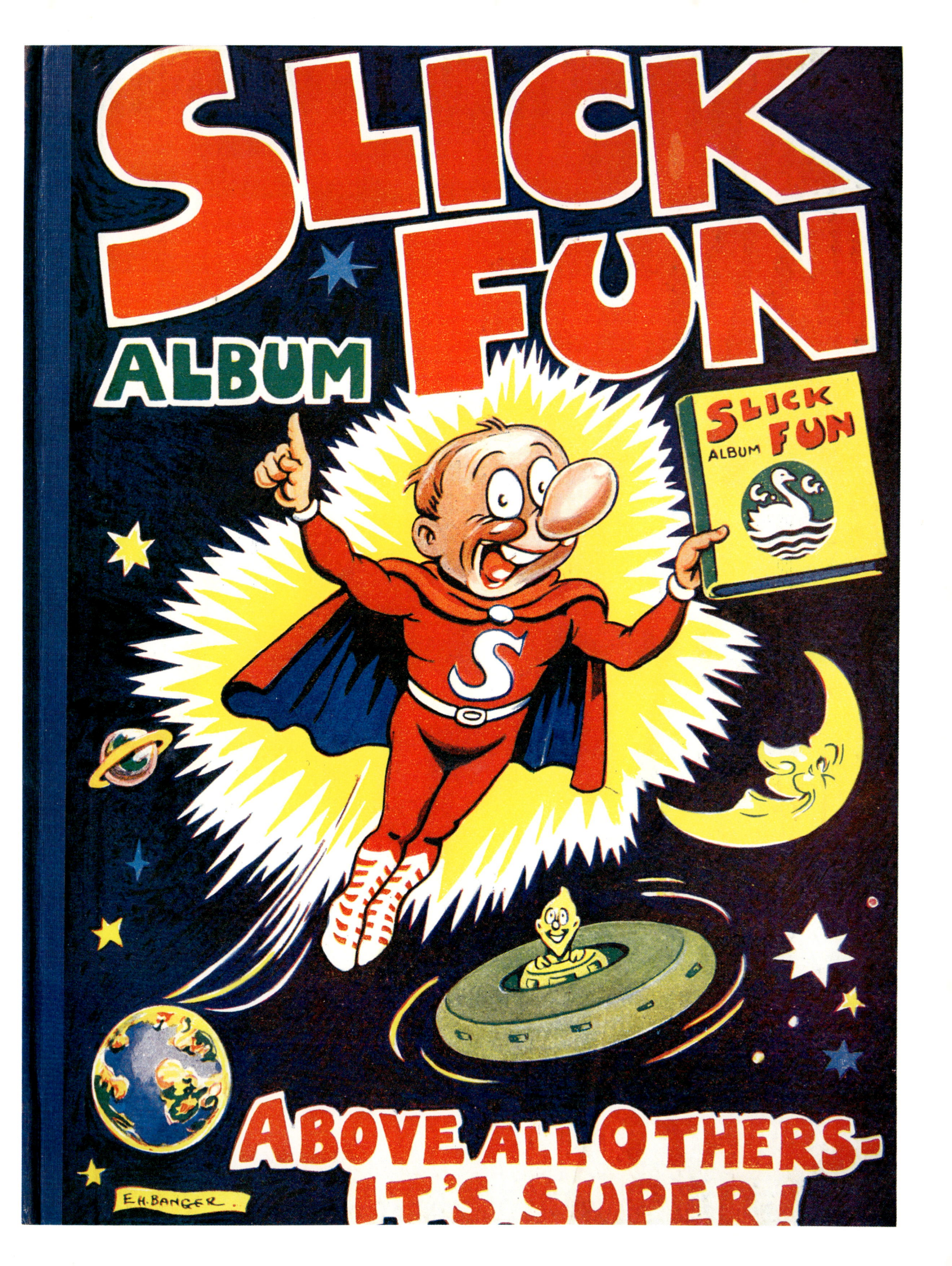

SLICK FUN ALBUM

ABOVE ALL OTHERS — IT'S SUPER!

E.H.BANGER

CAPTAIN UNIVERSE: THE SUPER MARVEL

by Mick Anglo
Captain Universe **(1954)**
Arnold Book Company (London)

'Working in the research laboratories of the United Nations Interplanetary Division, Jim Logan discovers an amazing secret. He treats himself electronically and thereafter, whenever he shouts the word "Galap", electronic impulses from outer space vibrate through him, endowing him with superhuman powers. He becomes Captain Universe, the Super Marvel!' Thus the foreword. A second box explained the magic word 'Galap':

G – for Galileo, Master of the Galaxies
A – for Archimedes, Master of Physics
L – for Leonardo da Vinci, Master of Invention
A – for Aristotle, Master of Philosophy
P – for Pythagoras, Master of Geometry

Which explained just about everything, except how Captain Universe managed to support a second subtitle, 'King of the Spaceways'. The Captain's debut adventure was entitled 'The Horror Plant of Coactus'. Strange tubes have fallen on Earth, tubes made of an unknown substance so heavy that a crane is needed to lift each one. Suddenly each tube grew into a full-size space ship and out came curious creatures from planet Coactus, crying 'Acko! We wreck!', to which the answer was 'Wacko! No tarf!' Jim Logan shouts his wonderful word and with a flashing *'Zwish!'* becomes Captain Universe. The Coactus-ites respond with 'Hacki-wacki! Slappi him happi!' and the fight is on. A trip to the centre of the Earth solves the problem. The Fanikins of Coactus, the Compressible Planet, can't stand heat!

Captain Universe, a slap-happy mixture of fun and fantasy, was another Mick Anglo creation, a fact revealed by the hero's typical anagrammatical surname, Logan. The comic also included Rocky Colt, a cowboy hero, and Lieut. Mike Miller of Homicide, another name full of clues. Mike was a variant of Mick, whilst Miller was the surname of publisher Arnold of the Arnold Book Company.

CAPTAIN UNIVERSE

An ABc Publication No. 1

6ᴅ

THE SUPER MARVEL

FEATURING
MIKE MILLER DETECTIVE
ROCKY COLT WESTERN

THE HORROR PLANT OF COACTUS

KING OF THE SPACEWAYS.....

MARVELMAN: THE MIGHTIEST MAN IN THE UNIVERSE

by Mick Anglo
Marvelman (1954)
L. Miller & Son Ltd (London)

'A recluse Astro-Scientist discovers the key word to the Universe, one that can only be given to a boy who is completely honest, studious, and of such integrity that he would only use it for the powers of good. He finds such a boy in Micky Moran, a newspaper copy boy, and treats him in a special machine which enables him to use the secret. Just before the scientist dies he tells Micky the key word, which is *"Kimota!"* Micky Moran stays as he was, but when he says the word he becomes Marvelman, a man of such strength and powers that he is invincible and indestructible.' This lengthy printed foreword preceded what would eventually become hundreds of adventures of Marvelman who, if he failed to prove the Mightiest Man in the Universe, certainly became the Mightiest Man in British Comics. His ten-year career was unprecedented and remain unequalled in strip history. The secret key word was, of course, based on a backward reading of the word 'atomic', and whenever Micky uttered it, 'Atomic strength smashes down to change Micky into mighty Marvelman', accompanied, of course, by an atomic cloud and the explosive word, *'Woof!'* Marvelman's first case, 'Marvelman and Atomic Bomber', appeared in No. 25 of *Marvelman*, which was actually No. 1, the first twenty-four issues being entitled *Captain Marvel*, an American reprint.

The actual as opposed to comic-book creation of Marvelman was a stop-gap action to continue the publication of Miller's successful weekly reprint of *Captain Marvel Adventures*. When the American publishers, Fawcett, gave up the comic rather than continue with a long-running lawsuit brought by their rival, D.C. Comics, Miller was left stranded. Artist Mick Anglo quickly took various elements of Captain Marvel and changed them into the new super-hero, Marvelman. Many artists worked on the long-running series, including the tyro Don Lawrence (illustrated), and yours truly!

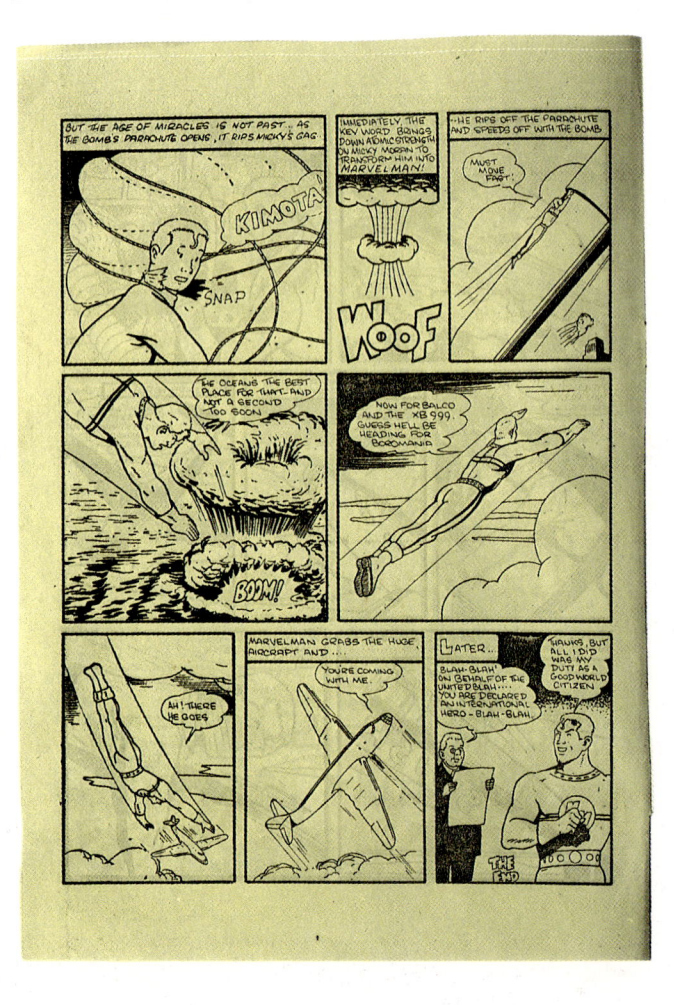

MARVELMAN

THE MIGHTIEST MAN IN THE UNIVERSE

L. MILLER & SON LTD LONDON

Vol. 1 No. 25

Price 6d

MARVELMAN AND THE ATOMIC BOMBER

MARVELMAN AT WAR

Marvelman comic-book No. 212 (7 September 1957) had an unusual announcement on the coloured cover:
Top Secret! At last we are able to release stories of Marvelman's thrilling wartime exploits! Look out for this smashing new series, 'Marvelman At War', starting next week... and here is a sample of the treats in store for you...

The cover story, 'Marvelman and the Coward', opened with a wartime splash panel, and told how Marvelman travelled back through time to the Ardennes in World War Two to prove Dave Brooks, a fellow staffer on the *Daily Bugle*, innocent of a charge of cowardice. This acted as a taster, and the following week, No.213 of the comic-book bore the brand new title of *Marvelman At War!* Subtitled 'Marvelman's Experiences in World War Two', the book bore a brand new insignia as well, and the lead story, 'The Commando Raid', was given the File Number of X27-1. The author was given for the first time, Rick Cassidy, yet another pen-name for Mick Anglo, who claimed 'All these stories are based on fact!'

Most surprising of all was to read that the adventure began in early 1941 in the office of the *Daily Bugle*, with Ed the editor looking exactly as he had been doing in 1957, and the same young Micky Moran, still a forelocked teenage copy-boy! The story that followed was set in Maagsoe, Norway, and was excellently illustrated by Don Lawrence.

MARVELMAN AT WAR

TOP SECRET FILE...X27-1
Vol 3 No 213
Week Ending September 14th 1957

★ Marvelman's experiences in World War Two!

Published by L. MILLER & SON LTD LONDON

The COMMANDO RAID

MARVELMAN ANNUAL

Nine annual editions of the *Marvelman Annual* were published from Christmas 1954 to 1963. The first book was produced with a soft card cover in a large page size, but standard hardback issues followed from 1956. The first annual contained 100 pages and was printed throughout in two colours, red and blue. The later books contained both black-and-white and full colour pages, and mixed strips with text stories. The last two annuals changed title to *Marvelman Adventures*. A popular feature of the annuals was the special game which featured the Mightiest Man in the Universe.

Editors for the series were W. T. Knott, Anthony Miller, Ann Colville and D.W. Boyce.

MARVELMAN ANNUAL

STRIP CARTOONS ★ STORIES
GAMES ★ PUZZLES ★ RIDDLES

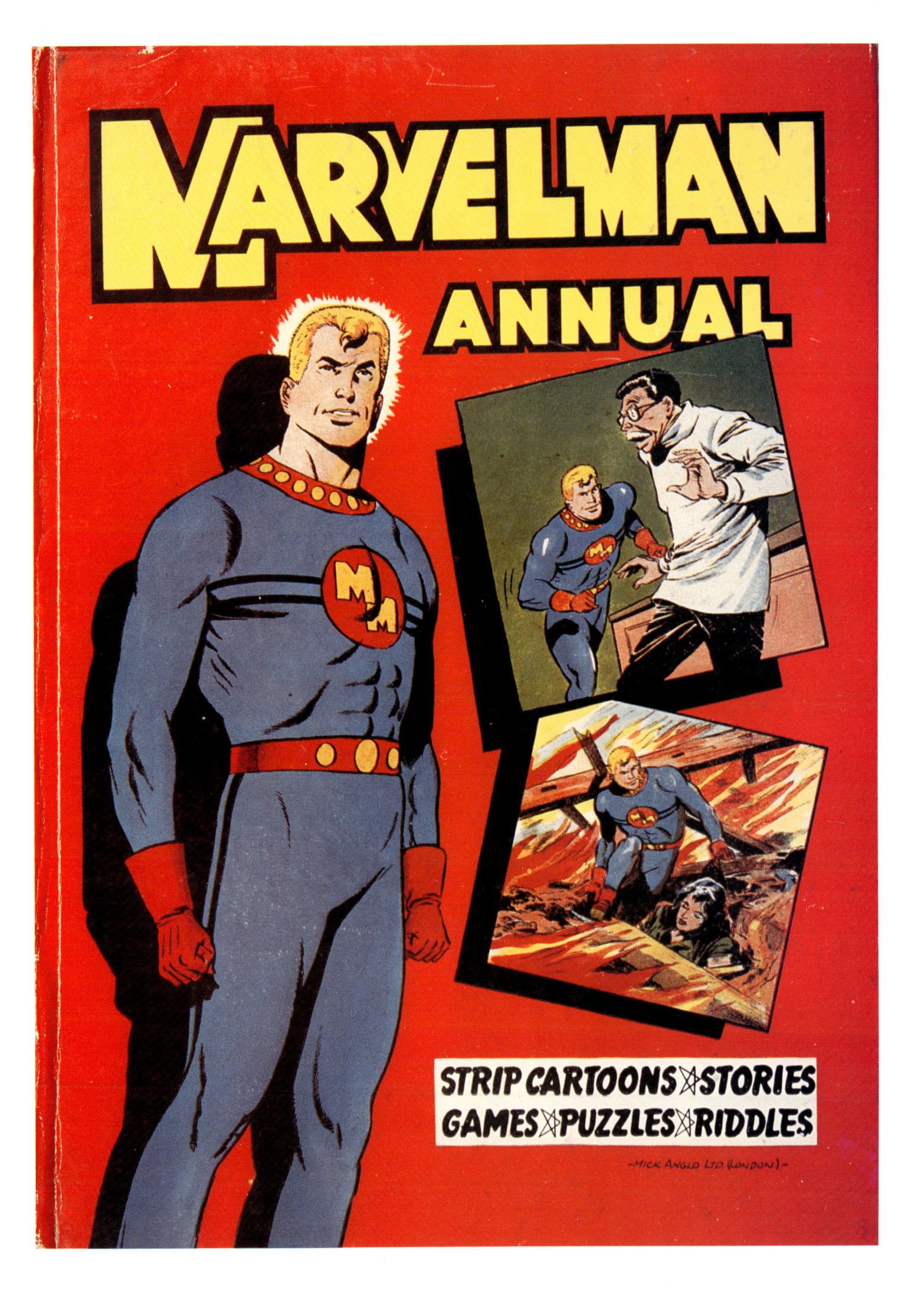

—MICK ANGLO LTD. (LONDON)—

YOUNG MARVELMAN: THE MIGHTIEST BOY IN THE UNIVERSE
by George Parlett
Young Marvelman (1954)
L. Miller & Son (London)

A somewhat flatly factual foreword introduced the first episode of Young Marvelman: 'Marvelman has given orphan Dicky Dauntless, whose hero he is, the power to assume the form of Young Marvelman, the Mightiest Boy in the Universe, by shouting the name – Marvelman!' Dicky, a uniformed messenger boy, works for the Transatlantic Messenger Service, under orders of the testy head, Silas Slocum. His first adventure, 'The Robot Bandit', has hardly begun when Dicky sees a sidewalk fracas. 'Holy Macaroni!' he cries, using his super-hero's favourite expletive, 'Marvelman!' The name brings atomic strength crashing down with the usual '*Woof!*', transforming Dicky into Young Marvelman. Wearing a similar skin-tight costume, save for a 'YM' where his hero wears a 'MM', the lithe youth swings into action: 'Taste some of this knuckle pie, pal,' he cries ('*Slam!*') adding, 'and an extra large portion for you, pal!' with his left ('*Whop!*'). But this is a mere overture, for evil Slim Spencer, hiding out at Gallows Tree Farm, has created a giant robot called Magno to do his future bank robberies! Balahoo City trembles as Magno steals ten million dollars in his first raid. But Young Marvelman is on his trail: 'Okay, Tinribs, here comes trouble!' And it sure does – '*Slam! Zam! Clang! Zonk! Zung! Blamm!*'

Young Marvelman began with issue No. 25, the previous twenty-four being reprints of *Captain Marvel Junior*, an American series suspended after a long lawsuit in the States. It meant a new career in comics for George Parlett, veteran of the Amalgamated Press comics where he had worked since the 1920s. His comedy-based style coupled with an ability to draw virtually anything and everything, proved perfect for the new Miller-Mick Anglo comic-book.

THE MIGHTIEST BOY IN THE UNIVERSE
YOUNG
MARVELMAN
PUBLISHED WEEKLY
WEEK ENDING JULY 24th, 1954
L. MILLER & SON LTD LONDON
6D
VOL I No 49
PRICE IN AUSTRALIA and NEW ZEALAND
8d
YOUNG
MARVELMAN
AND THE
LIFE STONE

YOUNG MARVELMAN ANNUAL

Nine annual editions of the *Young Marvelman Annual* were published from Christmas 1954 to 1962. The first of these gift books was produced with a soft card cover in a large page size, but standard hardback editions followed from 1955. The first annual contained 100 pages and was printed throughout in two colours, red and blue. The later books contained both black-and-white and full colour pages, and mixed strips with text stories. The last edition was retitled *Young Marvelman Adventures*. It was followed in 1963 with an inexplicable change of title to *Marvelman Junior*. A popular feature of the annuals was the inclusion of special games starring the Mightiest Boy in the Universe.

Editors for the series were W. T. Knott, Anthony Miller, Ann Colville and D.W. Boyce.

YOUNG MARVELMAN ANNUAL

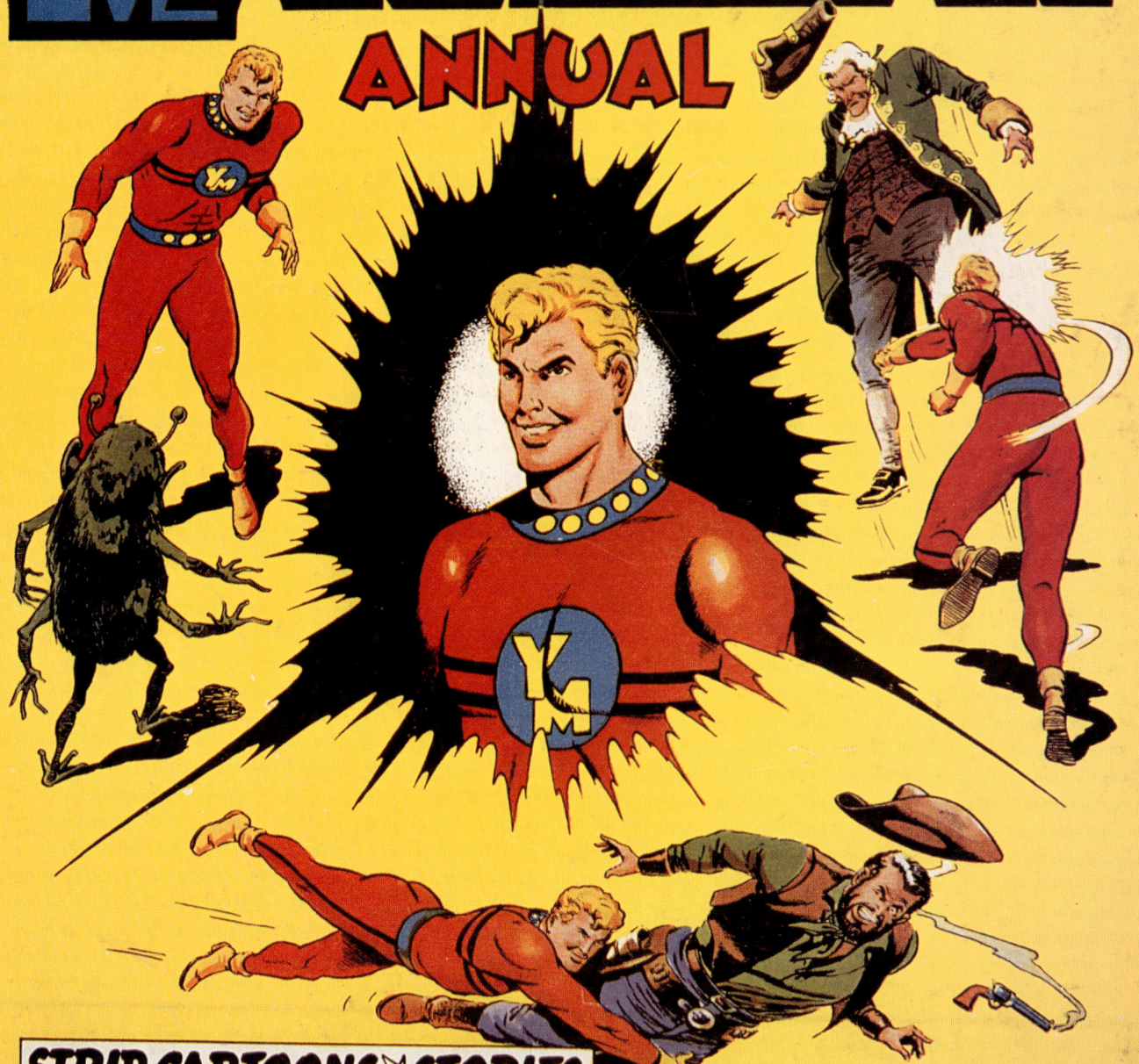

**STRIP CARTOONS ★ STORIES
GAMES ★ PUZZLES ★ RIDDLES**

— MICK ANGLO LTD. (LONDON) —

MARVELMAN FAMILY: THE MIGHTIEST FAMILY IN THE UNIVERSE

by Don Lawrence
Marvelman Family **(1956)**
L. Miller & Son (London)

The Marvelman Family was made up of Marvelman, Young Marvelman and Kid Marvelman, a trio which combined in 'The Invaders of the Future', the lead story in No.1 of their own comic-book, published October 1956. Kid Marvelman, however, had been introduced in No.102 of *Marvelman*, published 30 July 1955. Kid was really young Johnny Bates, a scrub-haired lad in striped tee-shirt and jeans, who was enlisted by Marvelman to help fight for justice and fair play. Johnny, who tended to cry 'Holy Balony!' instead of the usual Marvelman trademark of 'Holy Macaroni!', had but to shout the name of his hero for atomic power to come crashing down with the usual *'Woof!'* to change him into Kid Marvelman (insignia on chest, 'KM'). After several short back-up strips running four pages or so, the threesome combined in the new monthly comic-book to beat off Garrer and his army who invade Earth from the year 30,100 AD. They achieve this by travelling forward into time and thwarting the invasion at source.

This third comic-book in the *Marvelman* series was designed to substitute for the American reprints of *Marvel Family*. Whilst Marvelman substituted for Captain Marvel, and Young Marvelman for Captain Marvel Junior, editor Mick Anglo felt that a British equivalent of Mary Marvel would not attract his young boy readership. Thus Kid Marvelman was born, and established with occasional appearances in the parent comic-book, *Marvelman.* The *Family* comic was destined to run thirty monthly editions.

THE MIGHTIEST FAMILY IN THE UNIVERSE

Published by
L. MILLER
& SON LTD
LONDON

MARVELMAN FAMILY

No. 13

6D

THE OLYMPIC GAMES

MARVELMAN FAMILY ANNUAL

There was only one edition of the *Marvelman Family* as a hardbacked Christmas Annual. This was issued in 1963 as an economical, slender book of sixty-four pages, mostly black-and-white with sixteen pages printed (in the Netherlands!) in full colour. It contained only one Marvelman Family story, 'The Shadow Stealers', backed up with three Marvelman stories. Artwork was by Don Lawrence, who also drew the cover.

MARVELMAN Family
THE MIGHTIEST MAN IN THE UNIVERSE
Published by L. MILLER & Co. (HACKNEY) LTD.
STRIP CARTOONS
FEATURES
STORIES ★ PUZZLES

CAPTAIN MIRACLE
by Don Lawrence
Captain Miracle **(1960)**
Mick Anglo Ltd (London)

Remember Micky Moran, the blond young copy boy of the *Daily Bugle*? He had simply to shout the atomic key word, *'Kimota!',* for an atomic cloud to crash down and change him into Marvelman, Mightiest Man in the Universe! Well, folks, now meet Johnny Dee, black-haired editorial assistant of the *Daily Clarion*, who has simply to shout the magic words *'El Karim!'* for the magic Eastern formula to change him into the Formidable Captain Miracle! As they used to say in a certain radio series, 'Sounds Familiar...' With the over-worked *'Woof!'* changed to a *'Zip!',* and his chest emblem changed from 'MM' to a lightning flash, Captain Miracle was literally a new life for dear old Marvelman, with the old Don Lawrence strips from the Fifties partially redrawn by Mick Anglo for the Sixties.

Captain Miracle ran for nine monthly issues, including a title change on No. 6 to *Invincible*. Produced by Mick Anglo from his Hampstead Road Studio, this was one of a series of four 'Anglo Features' comic-books which were reworkings of strips originally produced by him for various L. Miller publications. Thus we have the extraordinary situation of Captain Marvel becoming Marvelman becoming Captain Miracle! The other three comic-books were *Battle*, *Gunhawks* and *TV Features*, all of them being distributed by Atlas Publishing Co. of Bride Lane.

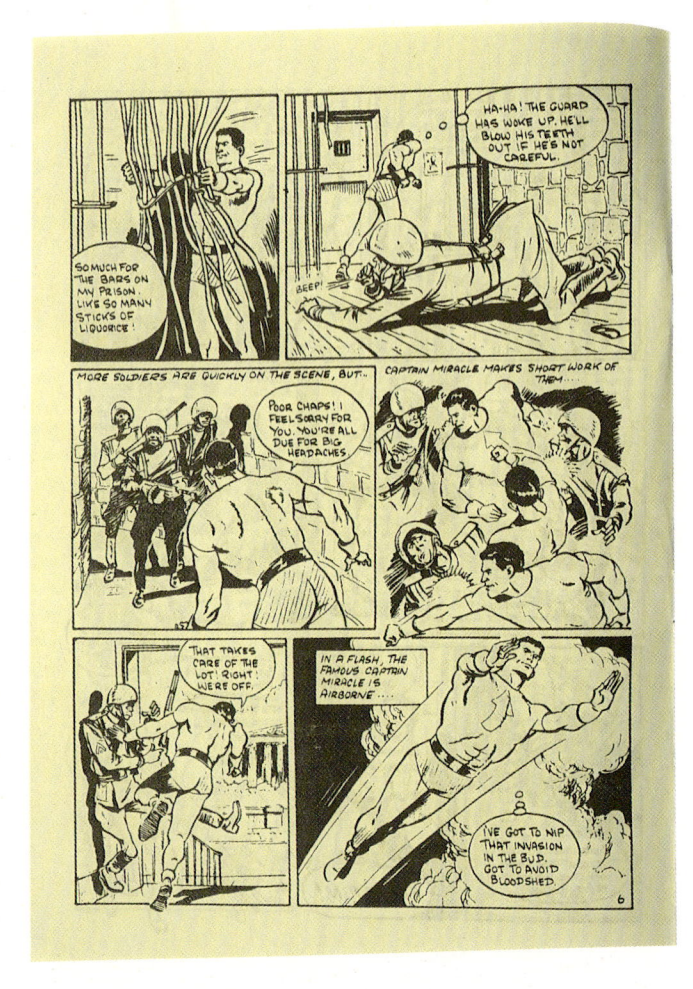

HERE IS YOUR FAVOURITE!

CAPTAIN MIRACLE
ALL STRIP CARTOON ADVENTURES

ANGLO FEATURES

No. 1

6ᴅ

THE PURPLE HOOD: CRIME FIGHTER INTERNATIONAL

by Michael Jay
The Purple Hood (1967)
John Spencer & Co (London)

All Lee Briton had to do to become the Purple Hood was to put on his super-suit, the mask-like headpiece of which completely covered his face, save for the eyes, climb into his mini-helicopter, spend half an hour flying to the London headquarters of Sir Franklyn James, head of a Top Secret Government Organisation, get his orders and start punching. The fight sequences, labelled *'Pow! Thump!'* and occasionally *'Thtoom!'*, appeared dynamic enough, but it slowly began to dawn that really this super-hero was not exactly super after all. However, his several adventures, beginning with 'The Fox on the Prowl', a tale of a modern Guy Fawkes planning to blow up the Houses of Parliament with an atom bomb, filled all fifty-two pages of the first shilling comic-book to star a British super-hero, so the Purple Hood certainly deserves a place in strip cartoon history.

The scripts for Michael Jay's illustrations were written by Gerald Wood. Publisher John Spencer was more at home with science-fiction paperbacks, but in 1967 produced a series of six shilling comic-books in the fantastic genre. These included *Macabre*, *Strange* and *Spectre*.

ALL ORIGINAL COMIC

NO. 1
1/-

LEE BRITON ALIAS

THE PURPLE HOOD

CRIME FIGHTER INTERNATIONAL!!

FEATURED INSIDE
THE FOX ON THE PROWL!

START FOLLOWING THE TERRIFIC EXPLOITS OF THIS FABULOUS CRIME FIGHTER TO END ALL CRIME FIGHTERS!!!

Michael Jayo

MARK TYME: THE FANTASTIC TIME TRAVELLER

by Michael Jay
Mark Tyme **(1967)**
John Spencer & Co (London)

The rain was pouring down in torrents outside, but Mark Tyme was oblivious to it as he donned his special costume for the first time. 'The material has a micro-thin skin of Gyptonian between the two layers of cloth, to act as a thermostat on the body,' he mused, 'to keep my body at correct temperature regardless of time or space.' For Mark had made a Time Machine! 'The main transporter is this hyper-dimensional computer,' he explained to himself, strapping on his wristwatch device. 'By pressing this button, it impulse signals back to this control, and so reverses the time process bringing me back to this day and age!' As the only way to test the Time Machine was to test it on himself, Mark sat down in the Electronic Triangle and started to flick the numerous coloured switches. 'Impulse beam rising,' he said as things went *'Wwrrrrrr!'* and *'Click-click!'* 'Slight tingling sensation in body,' he added as he began to disappear. Suddenly Mark was in a strange velvet void: 'My God! Have I flung myself into an endless void?' he cried. But no, he landed with a bump in Roman Britain! He looked at his watch; it said 41 BC! Further adventures in his first comic took Mark to 12,000 BC and Brighton, 1740. There were punch-ups everywhere!

Mark Tyme was a companion comic-book to *The Purple Hood*, also illustrated throughout by Michael Jay. Although both were well-drawn comics, neither survived past a second issue, and indeed hung about the bookshops so long that they had to be relabelled with the decimal price of '5p'.

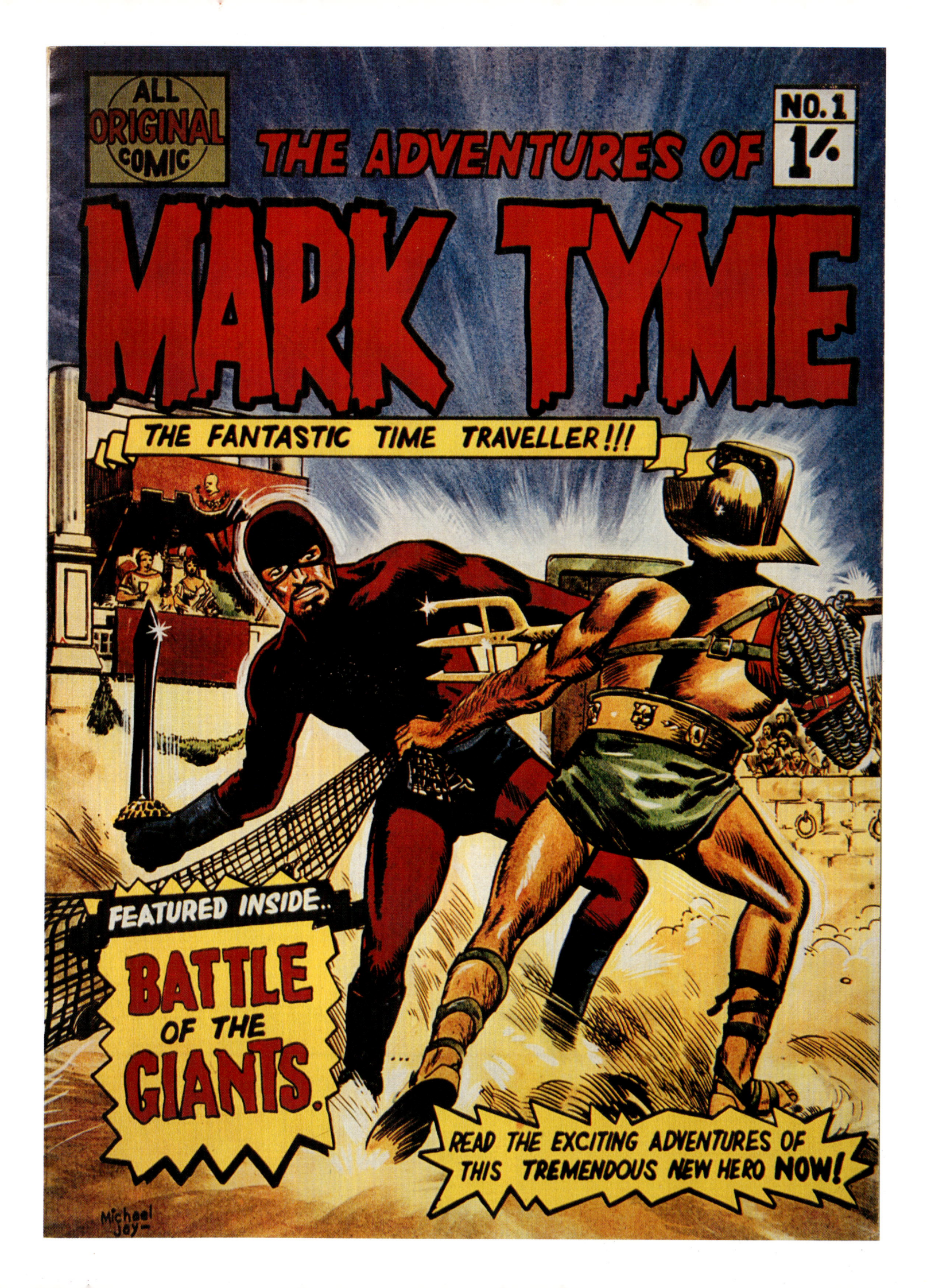

Amazing Comics ©1949 Modern Fiction Ltd
The Atom © 1947 Buchanan Books
Big Flame Wonder Comic © 1948 Scion Ltd
Big Game Comic © 1948 Scion Ltd
Big Win Comic © 1948 Scion Ltd
Bob Comic © 1949 Philmar Ltd
Captain Miracle © 1960 Anglo Features
Captain Universe © 1954 Arnold Book Co.
Captain Vigour © 1952 Sports Cartoons Ltd
Captain Zenith © 1950 Martin & Reid Ltd
Comic Capers © 1942 A. Soloway Ltd
Crash Comics © 1948 Rayburn Productions
Crasho Comics © 1947 W. Daly
Dynamic Thrills © 1952 Gerald G. Swan Ltd
Electroman Comics © 1951 Scion Ltd
Ensign Comic © 1947 Ensign Publications
Mark Tyme © 1967 John Spencer
Marsman Comics © 1948 Cartoon Art Productions
Marvelman © 1954 L. Miller & Son Ltd
Marvelman Annual © 1954 L. Miller & Son Ltd
Marvelman Family ©1956 L. Miller & Son Ltd

Marvelman Family Annual © 1963 L. Miller & Son Ltd
Masterman Comic © 1952 United Anglo-American Book Company
Oh Boy! Comics © 1948 Paget Publications
Picture Epics © 1952 Gerald G. Swan Ltd
Prang Comics © 1948 Hotspur Publishing Co.
Purple Hood © 1967 John Spencer
Red Flash Comic ©1948 Philmar Ltd
Rocket Comic © 1948 P.M. Productions
The Round-up © 1948 Children's Press
Slick Fun Album © 1956 Gerald G. Swan Ltd
Speed Gale Comics © 1947 Cartoon Art Productions
Steve Samson © 1953 Sports Cartoons Ltd
Streamline Comics © 1947 Cardal Publishing Co
Super Duper Comics © 1946 Cartoon Art Productions
Super Thriller © 1948 Foldes Press
Super Thriller Annual © 1959 World Distributors Ltd
Three Star Adventures © 1947 R. Turvey
Thrill Comics © 1942 Gerald G. Swan Ltd
Young Marvelman © 1954 L. Miller & Son Ltd
Young Marvelman Annual © 1954 L. Miller & Son Ltd